the MAKE AHEAD VEGAN
· COOKBOOK ·

125 FREEZER-FRIENDLY RECIPES

the MAKE AHEAD VEGAN
· COOKBOOK ·

125 FREEZER-FRIENDLY RECIPES

GINNY KAY MᶜMEANS

The Countryman Press
A division of W. W. Norton & Company
Independent Publishers Since 1923

The Countryman Press
www.countrymanpress.com

A division of W. W. Norton & Company, Inc.,
500 Fifth Avenue, New York, NY 10110
www.wwnorton.com

For information about special discounts for bulk purchases, please contact W. W. Norton Special Sales at specialsales@wwnorton.com or 800-233-4830.

Printed in China

Library of Congress Cataloging-in-Publication Data

McMeans, Ginny Kay, author.
  The make ahead vegan cookbook :
125 freezer-friendly recipes / Ginny Kay McMeans.
      pages cm
  "Independent Publishers Since 1923."
  Includes index.
  ISBN 978-1-58157-304-6 (hardcover)
  1. Vegan cooking. 2. Make-ahead cooking. I. Title.
  TX837.M47755 2016
  641.5'636—dc23
                              2015031019

10 9 8 7 6 5 4 3 2 1

DEDICATION

Dedicated to my mother, Vivian Kay,
who was my life's inspiration.

CONTENTS

CHAPTER THREE

TO WARM YOU FROM THE INSIDE OUT 97

CHAPTER FOUR

SIDE DISHES TO COMPLEMENT 127

CHAPTER FIVE
HEARTY MEALS 171

CHAPTER SIX
EXTRA EMBELLISHMENTS 221

INTRODUCTION

Comfort foods bring up thoughts of happy memories and have a place in all the cultures of the world. Often they are classics with just a small tweak for a regional twist, or they may be any staple that just makes you feel good. Dive into this cookbook for a variety of recipes that will have you conjuring up nostalgic happiness.

The Make Ahead Vegan Cookbook came about because of my desire to share all of the recipes that I have created and adapted over my years of cooking. Freezing delicious and healthy meals ranks high so that time is never an excuse for not eating well. There is a sensible and creative side to me that makes me want to serve vegan recipes that everyone loves. Yes, *everyone*, not just vegans. Nothing is more satisfying to me than to have people marveling over a Moist and Extravagant Carrot Bundt Cake or a very easy Slow Cooker Mushrooms and Rice recipe where the word *vegan* is never spoken. The recipes are just that good.

Cooking has always been one of my passions. I used to joke that I have made 3,000 different recipes—nowadays I think I actually have. It felt like a different meal every night and I loved it! When I first became vegan, I bought some cookbooks and did not realize that I had obtained some down-and-dirty, no-nonsense, hardcore vegan cookbooks that took no prisoners. There were lots of recipes that I wanted to re-create, but I literally had no idea what some of the ingredients were. With some Googling, I learned a lot of things and one of them is that I had to go to specialized grocery stores to source the products. Right away it was fun finding new foods to cook with and also learning how important it is to make sure I was getting all the vitamins and nutrition that I needed.

More knowledge was gained as I continued experimenting. And one of the big lessons I learned is that you really do *not* need many hard-to-find or specialty ingredients (or, at least, not very often). Grocery stores have come a long way since my first vegan days and I can find almost everything I need right here in my own small town. Chia seeds and coconut oil are sitting right there on the shelf. There are still some things that I need from specialty stores, such as full-fat coconut milk to make vegan ice cream, or nutritional yeast because it is such a great addition to so many recipes. Most of the basics for my recipes are fruits, vegetables, nuts, and grains obtained at the regular grocery store and local farmers' market. There seems to be organic everything, everywhere. You will also be amazed how many vegan products are already at your grocer's. A few of my recipes contain all-around, well-loved packaged items that are popular with everyone, everywhere.

For the purist at heart, I often offer alternatives in the recipe for people who don't want to use the store-bought brands. Instead of empanada disks, you can make your own homemade vegan dough. Take your choice. It is all vegan and freezer-friendly. A growing trend that I am seeing is that many people would like to make their own food from scratch, so that what they eat is as clean and natural as possible. My Italian Cannellini Soup is made with fresh ingredients and is to die for. No preservatives or additives, not ever. And did I also say: it's freezable!

An important factor that I think a lot of people miss is freezing their food. Everything I have mentioned can be frozen. It isn't hard. Freezing food is just something that needs to be pointed out and brought to the front of people's minds. When you freeze food, nothing is wasted. Freezing food is a daily routine in my life. Either things are going in or things are coming out. This cookbook will explain how you can easily make dishes, sides, and snacks that are delicious and also easy to freeze. Quality and nutrition will be preserved and you will have wonderful food at your fingertips. Freezing recipes is not labor intensive as some might think and my recipes are tried and true. I want people to understand this and also reap the benefits.

If you want to save time in the kitchen, you can turn that one meal into two by just doubling your ingredients and packaging some for the freezer. That is such a satisfying feeling! Breakfast, lunch, or dinner—there can always be something in the freezer that will defrost in no time or that you can zap in the microwave. You don't need a large freezer or an extra full-size freezer in the garage to cook this way—although that would be fun.

I have one of those white refrigerators with the freezer on top—you know the kind—and it is not even full. Sometimes it fills up, but when it gets there I am reminded to kick back and eat some of those delicious and nutritious meals inside, such as the Panini Chili Bean Cakes, American Tetrazzini, or those Five-Spice Comfort Pita Sandwiches. "Wow!" I think to myself, "I just got a few days off."

Here is something else that I tackled when I became a vegan: How could I turn my most beloved recipes into their vegan cousins, and still keep intact the flavors I loved? My experimenting began by exchanging a nonvegan ingredient for a vegan one, and new recipes were born. I discovered you can make a deep, rich French onion soup with no beef stock.

And, did you know that most raw fruit balls or date balls and cookie dough treats can all be frozen? They can even be eaten right out of the freezer. That was a pleasant discovery!

Exciting flavors are abundant throughout this book. It has been my goal to create the most flavorful recipes possible that can be enjoyed not only by the vegan community but also by nonvegans everywhere. People from every part of the country have been in touch with me to say they love my recipes, and I love to get these compliments because it assures me that my goal is being accomplished.

THE NITTY-GRITTY OF FREEZING

To Freeze or Not to Freeze

It is a major factor to decide what to freeze or not to freeze. Luckily, almost everything can be frozen. This is going to be a very short discussion. A blanket category of things that don't freeze well is dairy items. That won't be a problem with my recipes because I do not use any dairy.

ITEMS NOT TO FREEZE

- *Potatoes often become mealy.* An exception is mashed potatoes; they freeze beautifully. When I do soups or stews, I parboil the potatoes right before dinner and put them in the defrosted recipe when heating for the meal.
- *Raw produce with a high water content,* such as cabbage, celery, cucumber, eggplant, endive, fennel, leafy greens, lettuce, parsley, peppers, radishes, ripe tomatoes, summer squash, turnips, watermelons, and zucchini, become soggy if frozen.
- *Many herbs and spices* change their flavor when frozen. I will tell you which herb or spice to add later in each of my recipes.

Containers for Freezing Food

There's a wide variety of containers for freezing food, from plastic to glass from flimsy to rigid. I use all of them and here is a description of each type and my favorites.

- Glass containers with airtight lids
- Glass containers with lids that are not airtight
- Glass canning jars that are made for freezing (read the packaging). The only ones I have found are wide-mouth jars. None have been over the size of a pint, either.
- Plastic, lidded, rigid-sided containers that are not airtight
- Freezer bags from the grocery store, in different sizes
- Aluminum foil. This works in some situations.

The glass containers with airtight lids are very easy. All you do is put your food inside and snap on the lids. They do take up a bit more space in the freezer, but they stack so neatly and I can move them much easier when looking for food.

Glass containers with lids that are not specifically made for the freezer are great for ease also, but they are not airtight, so you will need to slide the whole container into a freezer bag. I point out a handy technique in "Preparing Food for the Freezer" that will enable you to remove your empty casserole dish after the food is frozen.

Glass canning jars are also easy. You just need to remember to leave about an inch of space between the food and the lid because liquids expand when frozen. Do

not use cleaned-out jars that used to hold spaghetti sauce or other items, because they were not made for freezing and may break or not hold a good seal.

The heavier, lidded, plastic-sided containers that you buy new in the store will need to be slipped into a freezer bag.

Freezer bags will hold baked goods, other containers that are not airtight, liquids, and just about anything. They have zippered tops and can be used over and over. I do not try to save bags that held anything liquid, though. If the freezer bags are just holding closed containers, they are very simple to save. I save an older, empty freezer bag box, and after the freezer bags have dried out, I roll them, one at a time, and slide them back into the box. Nice and neat.

When freezing food in a freezer bag without a container, try to push out as much air as possible before sealing.

Aluminum foil can be used for wrapping around solids after they have already been prewrapped in plastic wrap. Otherwise, the foil could cause a reaction with some foods that it touches during storage.

Preparing Food for the Freezer

There are multiple ways in preparing food for the freezer. I quickly mentioned a few in the section "Containers for Freezing Food."

The easiest procedure and the one I use the most is to put food in freezer-safe glass containers that have four tabs all around on their plastic lids. These snap and give an airtight seal. My containers have been used numerous times and I see no end to their life.

Glass canning jars are equally easy. You just need to remember to leave about an inch of space between the liquid and the lid. Liquid expands and will have a higher level after it has frozen. I have only seen wide-mouth jars marked as freezer jars, and never in the quart size.

Many firm items—such as bean patties, berries, and certain sweets like truffles—can be frozen without a covering and then, within one to 10 hours, put into freezer bags. You lay them out, without touching, on a cookie sheet and then slide the sheet into the freezer. Allow the food to freeze until solid. This allows items to freeze without sticking together. You might have to use a spatula to pop them off the cookie sheet, but they come off very easily. Then, pop them into a freezer bag and they are done.

Sometimes I like to wrap my items individually with plastic wrap. This works well with such things as bean patties. When I am finished, I place the group of wrapped items in a freezer bag or rigid-sided plastic container with a lid. Just another option for when I am running low on my glass containers.

Casseroles come next. They can also be frozen in the glass containers with airtight lids—as is. When I am running low on containers, I will go to the little extra work to freeze in plastic wrap and freezer foil. First, I line the container with foil so that all corners are covered. Then I do the same thing with plastic wrap laid on top of the foil. I put my casserole into the prepared dish just as I would normally. The casserole is touching the plastic wrap, not the foil. Fold all the sides in, the plastic wrap first and then the foil. Label the foil clearly and slide into the freezer, in the glass container. After the casserole is solid, remove it from the glass dish and put the wrapped casserole back into the freezer. When you want to use this casserole, remove all the wrapping (both the foil and the plastic). Then slide the casserole back into the original casserole dish to defrost. Bake when defrosted as directed.

Another way that I have adopted for casseroles is to make two long handles with aluminum foil. The way you do this is to take a long strip of foil that is about twice as long as your casserole dish. Fold it over many times so it is one long, many-layered strip. Lay this in your casserole dish down the middle. Make your casserole as you normally would. Put this in the freezer to harden. When the food is solid, take the dish out of the freezer. Use the "handles" made of foil to carefully remove the food from the dish. Now pack this in a freezer bag (sliding out the foil handle) seal, and replace in the freezer. Now you have your casserole dish back.

Lastly, don't forget to label the items. It makes life so much easier. I use freezer tape and sometimes I write on the freezer bag with a permanent marker.

As you can see, you can find an option for every situation in preparing food for the freezer. It is so rewarding to open your freezer and have food for breakfast, lunch, dinner, and snacks just waiting for you.

Blanching Vegetables—Preparing Veggies Correctly for Freezing

Blanching vegetables is an easy step, but a necessary one, when you are planning to freeze fresh vegetables.

- Get a pot that is large enough to hold your vegetables and water to cover. While the water is coming to a boil, clean and prepare your vegetables.
- When the water is at a boil, plunge in your vegetables.
- Cover and set your timer (see blanching times) as soon as the water starts to boil again.
- Set up a big bowl of ice water for cooling down the vegetables.
- Drain the vegetables and immediately put into the bowl of ice water. Leave for a few minutes.
- Remove the vegetables from the cool water, lay out, and pat dry.
- Pack into your container of choice. All done.

This blanching method kills the enzymes to keep the veggies from spoiling. It also sets the color for freezing.

BLANCHING TIMES

Following is a list of blanching times (in minutes) for specific vegetables.

Asparagus	3
Bean sprouts	4
Black-eyed peas	2

Stocking the Freezer

Freezers are colder in some spots than in others. There are certain ways to pack a freezer to be more energy efficient. Stocking the freezer with store-bought items and homemade goods will give you a wide array of choices.

Your freezer temperature should be 0°F or lower.

By opening the freezer, we expose the door to air more often. That makes it a good place to put such items as breads and other baked goods.

The back of the freezer is a good option for larger items that are easier to be seen and won't get lost in the shuffle.

Don't pack your freezer full. You want to have some space for circulation. But with that in mind, the fuller you can keep it (with some air space), the better it is for saving energy. The solid frozen objects inside the freezer will keep it colder so the freezer won't have to work as hard. A freezer that is half-full will need to work harder to keep the temperature down.

It is great if you could keep a list taped to the inside of your pantry of what is inside your freezer. When you get home from grocery shopping, you can add items to the list. When you remove items to consume, just scratch them off.

If at all possible, keep items that are similar in the same areas. Put snacks together, breads together, casseroles, and so forth. That can be a little difficult. If I had a door down the side with more shelves for compartmentalizing, I think that might be a bit easier.

My husband has his favorite meals, as we all do. These are the items I will cook over and over, and I try to have one of them in the freezer at all times. There are also some dishes that are easier to prepare for eating. Especially those that fit into the glass containers with airtight lids. I will make sure a couple of these casseroles are in the freezer for my husband to cook in case I am gone a couple of days. He loves me for it and I aim to please.

Freezer Storage Times

Freezer storage time for food stands for the quality of the food. Items can be stored much longer and in some cases forever, but the flavor and texture will not be at its best.

Again, the freezer temperature should be 0°F or lower.

Soups ....5–6 months
Stews...5–6 months
Chili ....5–6 months
Pasta dishes...2–3 months

Side dishes	2–3 months
Casseroles	2–3 months
Spaghetti sauce	5–6 months
Muffins	2–3 months
Cakes	2–3 months
Quick breads	3–4 months
Yeast breads	3–4 months
Cookies	3–5 months
Pizza dough	8–9 months
Vegetables	8–9 months
Fruit	8–9 months

Tips and Tricks

Use quality products because that is the product you are going to get after it has been frozen. Bad food does not improve.

Remove soups and stews from the heat and then stir them every once in a while to help them cool more quickly for freezing.

Pack for the size family that you have. I always pack for two because it works for us. Pack 9 x 13-inch casseroles for a family of six or when company is coming. For easier handling (and for the long, side freezers that come with many refrigerators), pack duplicate 8- or 9-inch square dishes instead of one large, long casserole. I have done this, too, and I like it.

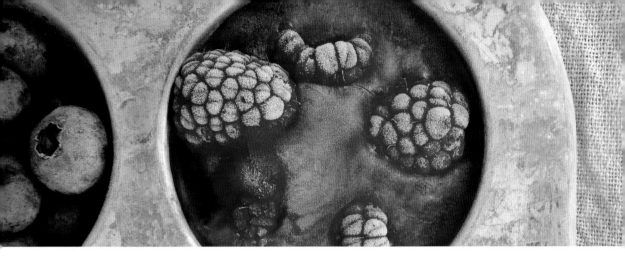

If you have the room, keep muffins and bars in the freezer. It makes breakfast so much easier. When you are running out the door, you can grab a nice healthful muffin from the freezer. They defrost in no time and are easy to tuck into a purse or bag.

Frozen waffles are wonderful. Pop them into the toaster and there you go.

Reuse your foil and bags. If they have not touched the food, just open to air dry on your counter.

Leftover pasta, without a sauce, freezes great. Let it cool to room temperature and drop it into a container to freeze. When you want to use it, bring some water to a boil to cover. Drop in the pasta and heat it through. It only takes about a minute and tastes fresh.

If cooking pasta for casseroles that will be baked in the oven later—cook it al dente. The pasta will finish cooking when you are baking the final product.

I put into small plastic containers (2- or 4-ounce sizes) certain items that I will need in small quantities at a later time. No food is wasted. Some examples are tomato paste, vegetable stock, and any red sauce. Then I put the small containers into one large freezer bag. The items inside will rotate as you use them.

Ice cube trays are wonderful for making tiny servings of flavors that you will need. After the cubes are frozen, remove them from the tray and put them in a freezer bag. Now, you can take out a cube or two. Some liquids I freeze in trays are lemon, orange, coffee, tea, and stocks.

Items that can defrost at room temperature are baked goods, such as bread, cookies, and cakes. Unwrap so they don't get soggy.

Thaw other foods in the refrigerator—never on the counter. Depending how large the solid mass is, this can take from 12 to 24 hours. My one exception to this rule is defrosting food in the microwave. Smaller items will defrost on the DEFROST setting, but they can also cook on the edges, so keep a close watch.

If you have a power failure, keep the freezer door closed as much as possible. A full freezer will keep good for 2 to 3 days and a half-full freezer will keep for 1 to 2 days. Food is still good and can be kept in the freezer if the temperature stays below 40°F.

For single side dishes, you can freeze rice and mashed potatoes in lined muffin cups. Remove from the muffin tins and put into freezer bags. When you want to serve, just remove an individual portion, take off the liner, put in a bowl, and heat in the microwave.

A little trick I use when we go traveling is that I half-fill a covered jar with water. I place it in the freezer and let it freeze. Before we leave on the trip, I lay it on its side. When we get home, if the ice is still in the bottom, then there was no problem. If the ice is on the side of the jar, then we had a long power failure.

Freezer burn is when your food turns a darker color and looks drier. It won't make you sick, but it won't taste very good, either. If the freezer burn is just around the corners, it can be cut off and the rest will still taste good. If it has gone further than that, then throw the entire item away.

If your food is cooked before you freeze it, make sure it is room temperature before putting it in the freezer. If it is too warm, that is how ice crystals are formed. A few crystals are inescapable, but you don't want to help cause freezer burn.

Freeze your leftovers if they have not been frozen before.

I always double my muffin batches to have one on hand and one to freeze. Then, no one in the house is ever tempted to buy the unhealthy packaged sweets when going shopping.

Another great way to freeze muffins is to actually put your muffin batter into lined muffin cups and freeze the tin without baking it. When the batter becomes solid, remove the unbaked muffins from the muffin tin and put them into a freezer bag. You don't need to defrost them before baking. Just preheat the oven, put them back into the muffin tin, and add 10 minutes to the baking time.

Freeze soups in small containers for single servings.

HELPFUL INFORMATION ABOUT EGG SUBSTITUTES

Many egg substitutes are available for baking or for use in recipes that call for eggs. A few egg replacers come in boxes and look like flour. These work really well and are found at any natural foods grocery store. Alternatively, usually one mashed banana or ¼ cup of applesauce also works to replace one egg. A tablespoon of ground flaxseed meal mixed with 3 tablespoons of warm water can be used as an egg as well. One substitute that I often use is a chia egg. It gels quickly and works really well. The way you get a chia egg is by grinding chia seeds to a fine meal. I have a coffee bean grinder that I use exclusively for chia flour. Then you mix 1 tablespoon of chia flour with 3 tablespoons of water. It gels almost immediately. Keep the chia meal in a freezer jar in the freezer and you can have an 'egg' for your recipes at a moment's notice.

CHAPTER ONE
Party Pleasers

Freezing:

After you have assembled your wontons on the baking sheet, just slide it in the freezer and let them freeze for about 1 hour. Remove with a metal spatula and store in a freezer-safe bag or in a hard-sided freezer container. I prefer the hard-sided way because the tips can break easily and then they won't be so pretty. To defrost, put in your refrigerator overnight.

Western Wontons

Wonton wrappers make the perfect small package for these spicy appetizers. You will get compliments for the visual and the taste.

YIELD: 48 WONTONS | **ACTIVE TIME:** 1 HOUR | **COOK TIME:** 20 MINUTES | **TOTAL TIME:** 1 HOUR 20 MINUTES

Heat 1 tablespoon of the coconut oil in a large skillet over medium heat. Add the onion and sauté for about 5 minutes. Next, add the red bell pepper and chile pepper, and sauté for another 5 minutes. Add the corn, beans, yeast, spices, salt, and black pepper, and heat through for about 3 minutes.

Work with two baking sheets so that you can be folding one set of wontons while the others are baking. Spread 1 to 2 teaspoons of the remaining coconut oil on each baking sheet. Lay out the wontons about an inch apart so that they fit comfortably on the sheet. Scoop about 2 teaspoons of the bean mixture into the center of each wonton.

Have a small bowl of water ready. Dip your finger in the water. Then wipe the edge of two opposite sides of a wrapper so that they are moist. This works as the "glue" and keeps the wontons closed perfectly. Fold over one point to meet the tip of the opposite point. This will make a triangle. Fold the three tips inside to protect them from burning. Press the edges down and firmly seal with your fingertip.

At this point you may freeze the wontons; otherwise, preheat the oven to 425°F.

Bake the wontons for 4 minutes, then flip over and bake for 3 more minutes—7 minutes total. If you don't fold the tips to the inside, which you don't have to, use a timer, because the tips can burn quickly.

Serve this flavorful little appetizer as is or with your favorite salsa for dipping.

3 tablespoons coconut oil, divided

½ cup white onion, diced small

½ cup red bell pepper, diced small

1 small chile pepper, seeded and finely diced

½ cup corn kernels, cut off a cob or frozen

1 (15-ounce) can black beans, drained and rinsed

2 teaspoons nutritional yeast

½ teaspoon ground cumin

¼ teaspoon chili powder

¼ teaspoon cayenne pepper

¼ teaspoon garlic powder

½ teaspoon salt

¼ teaspoon freshly ground black pepper

48 vegan pot sticker/wonton wrappers

Storing in the refrigerator:

These will keep for up to 3 days in the refrigerator.

Reheating:

To serve, microwave at medium power for 30 seconds. Redistribute the wontons and microwave for 30 more seconds. They will also be good at room temperature.

Garlic Hummus Stuffed Mini Cups

These substantial little bites have everything going for them. They are sturdy, flavorful, and look really good.

YIELD: ABOUT 20 MINI CUPS | **ACTIVE TIME:** 30 MINUTES | **COOK TIME:** 8 MINUTES | **TOTAL TIME:** 38 MINUTES

Preheat the oven to 400°F. Lightly grease about 20 mini muffin cups with coconut oil.

Roll out the dough to about 14 x 12 inches and cut circles with a round cutter that measures 1½ to 2 inches in diameter, depending what will fit in your mini muffin tins.

Lightly press each circle into a prepared muffin cup so that the dough molds to the sides and bottom. Bake for 8 minutes. Let cool completely.

Heat the coconut oil in a skillet over medium-high heat. Add the onion and bell pepper, and sauté for 5 minutes. Add the mushrooms and sauté for another 5 to 10 minutes.

Put a dollop of hummus into the center in each cup and sprinkle the top with the veggie mixture. Sprinkle the tiniest pinch of salt over the veggies.

1 tablespoon coconut oil, plus more for pan

1 recipe Whole Wheat Pastry Dough (recipe follows)

½ cup white onion, finely diced

1 red bell pepper, finely diced

8 ounces button mushrooms, diced

1 (8- to 10-ounce) container garlic hummus

Sea salt

Whole-Wheat Pastry Dough

¾ cup warm water (110°F)

1 tablespoon active dry yeast

2 cups plus 2 tablespoons whole wheat pastry flour, plus more for dusting

2 teaspoons pure maple syrup

1 tablespoon plus 1 teaspoon olive oil, divided

½ teaspoon salt

In a small bowl, add the yeast to the warm water. Stir and set aside.

In a large bowl, combine the flour, maple syrup, 1 tablespoon of the olive oil, and the yeast mixture.

Mix well and then turn out onto a lightly floured surface and gently knead into a smooth, firm ball.

Oil a large bowl with the teaspoon of olive oil.

Place the dough in the oiled bowl and turn the dough all around to get the oil on the whole ball.

Cover the bowl lightly with a clean towel and put it in a warm area to let it double in size, about 1 hour.

Roll out the dough and continue with the mini cup directions.

Storing in the refrigerator:

Store the cups, hummus, and topping separately in the refrigerator. Assemble the day of serving and then cover with plastic wrap.

Freezing:

The dough will keep in the freezer for up to 9 months. If you want to mold the dough cups and freeze them, they will keep in the freezer for 4 months. Hummus will keep for about 6 months. Do not freeze the topping. After defrosting the necessary ingredients, proceed assembly as described.

Mini Burritos

A perfect appetizer for picking up with your fingers. I would like to say there are three good bites, but I have witnessed people downing them in two.

YIELD: 24 BURRITOS | **ACTIVE TIME:** 45 MINUTES | **COOK TIME:** 10 MINUTES | **TOTAL TIME:** 55 MINUTES

Preheat the oven to 400°F. Lightly oil a baking sheet with 2 tablespoons of the coconut oil and set aside.

Heat the remaining tablespoon of coconut oil in a large skillet. Sauté the onion and bell pepper for about 5 minutes. Remove from the pan and let cool about 5 minutes. Place in a food processor and pulse smaller. Turn out the mixture into a medium-size bowl.

Add the mushrooms to the original sauté pan and sauté for about 15 minutes, then transfer to the vegetable mixture. Stir in the remaining ingredients, except the wrappers.

Lay the wrappers on a flat surface. Divide the filling equally among the 24 wrappers. Fold in two opposite sides of each wrapper and then roll up as a burrito. Place on the prepared baking sheet, seam side down, about 2 inches apart. Bake for 10 to 12 minutes, turning over halfway through. Serve with your favorite dipping salsa.

3 tablespoons coconut oil, divided

½ cup white onion, diced

½ cup green bell pepper, diced

8 ounces button mushrooms, cleaned and diced small

1 tomato, diced (about ½ cup)

½ (15-ounce) can pinto beans, drained and rinsed, or 1 cup cooked, lightly mashed

½ cup vegan panko

¼ teaspoon ground cumin

¼ teaspoon chili powder

Dash of Tabasco sauce

½ teaspoon salt

24 vegan pot sticker/wonton wrappers

Storing in the refrigerator:

The completed burritos will keep in a tightly sealed container in the refrigerator for 3 to 4 days.

Freezing:

You may store the completed burritos in a freezer-safe bag or a hard-sided freezer container. To defrost, put them in your refrigerator overnight.

Reheating:

To serve, heat in a 350°F oven for 10 minutes. They will be good at room temperature, too. Serve with a dipping salsa.

Mushroom Purses

Transparent wonton wrappers send an invitation to the flavorful bite that is inside. These pretty purses will make you feel as if you received two invitations.

YIELD: 24 TO 30 MUSHROOM PURSES | **ACTIVE TIME:** 15 MINUTES | **COOK TIME:** 30 MINUTES | **TOTAL TIME:** 45 MINUTES

Preheat the oven to 435°F. Lightly grease two baking sheets with coconut oil. Set aside.

Heat the coconut oil in a large skillet over medium-high heat. Add the mushrooms and cook for about 15 minutes, until they are cooked down and most of t he liquid is cooked out, adding the garlic during the last 5 minutes. Add the wine and cook over medium-high heat until the wine is almost evaporated. Turn out the mixture into a medium-size bowl. Add the tomatoes and seasonings. Mix well.

Lay out a couple of the wrappers. Place a teaspoon of the filling in the center of each wrapper.

Have a small bowl of water ready. Dip your finger in the water. Then wipe the edges of the wrapper so that they are moist. This works as the "glue" and keeps the wontons closed perfectly. Pick up two opposite points and meet them at the center, then pick up the other two opposite points to meet at the center. Now pinch the four sides from the point to the base so that they form a little "purse." (See the photo as an example.)

Place on the prepared baking sheet. When the baking sheet is full (probably 12 to15 purses), bake for 10 minutes. Watch closely because the tips can burn quickly toward the end. You do want then to turn a bit brown, though. Remove from the oven and let cool on a wire rack. Continue until all the filling is used.

Eat as a finger food as is or serve with hoisin sauce or another of your favorite Asian sauces, such as a Thai Sweet Hot Chili Sauce (page 228).

1 tablespoon coconut oil, plus more for baking sheets

2 pounds button mushrooms, diced small

4 cloves garlic, minced or finely diced

½ cup dry white wine, such as chardonnay

3 tablespoons oil-packed sun-dried tomatoes, chopped small

½ teaspoon dried basil

½ teaspoon sea salt

¼ teaspoon freshly ground black pepper

24 to 30 vegan pot sticker/wonton wrappers

Storing in the refrigerator:

The mushroom purses will keep in the refrigerator for 4 to 5 days.

Freezing:

You can store the mushroom purses in a hard-sided freezer container. This will better protect them. To defrost, put in your refrigerator overnight.

Reheating:

To serve, microwave about six at a time on high power for 15 to 20 seconds.

Spicy Stuffed Crescents

In preparation for the party, make your life easier by using packaged crescent rolls. These rolls are a crowd-pleaser whether they are dipped in salsa or not.

YIELD: 24 CRESCENTS | **ACTIVE TIME:** 35 MINUTES | **COOK TIME:** 10 MINUTES | **TOTAL TIME:** 45 MINUTES

Preheat the oven to 375°F.

Heat the coconut oil in a large skillet over medium heat.

Add the vegan beef and heat through, breaking up into tiny crumbles.

Add the cream cheese and blend into the beef. Add the cumin, chili powder, and garlic powder. Cook, stirring, for about 1 minute. Add the green chiles, black olives, and salt and pepper, and stir well to combine.

Remove from the heat. Roughly divide the mixture into 24 portions. In the skillet, divide the mixture in half, then divide those two halves in half. Then it will be easier to eyeball those four parts into sixths to get your 24 fillings. They will be about a heaping teaspoon each.

Work with one can of crescent rolls at a time. Open the can and spread out the eight crescent triangles. Put a dollop of the filling at the one end of a triangle. Roll up as you would for crescent rolls. Place all eight rolled-up crescents on a baking sheet. Bake for 11 minutes, or until golden brown.

Continue with the rest of the filling and crescents as described above.

NOTE:

Use low-fat crescent rolls, to avoid trans fats.

1 tablespoon coconut oil

1 (10-ounce) package vegan ground beef

1 ounce nondairy cream cheese

½ teaspoon ground cumin

½ teaspoon chili powder

¼ teaspoon garlic powder

1 (4-ounce) can chopped green chiles

1 (4-ounce) can chopped black olives

1 teaspoon salt

¼ teaspoon freshly ground black pepper

3 cans refrigerated vegan crescent rolls (see note)

Storing in the refrigerator:

The crescents will keep in the refrigerator for 3 to 4 days.

Freezing:

You may store the completed crescents in a freezer-safe bag or a hard-sided freezer container. To defrost, put them in your refrigerator overnight.

Reheating:

To serve, heat in a 350°F oven for 10 minutes. They will be good at room temperature, too.

Cauliflower Chickpea Pizza Bites

Cauliflower is such a versatile vegetable. Here it is combined with lots of complementing ingredients and baked into the shape of a mini muffin. So easy to pop in your mouth.

YIELD: 36 TO 48 MUFFINS | **ACTIVE TIME:** 40 MINUTES | **COOK TIME:** 30 MINUTES | **TOTAL TIME:** 1 HOUR 10 MINUTES

Preheat the oven to 350°F. Lightly oil 36 to 48 mini muffin cups with the coconut oil. Your output will depend on the size of the cauliflower head.

Cut the cauliflower into florets. Steam until the florets are easy to pierce, about 15 minutes. Transfer to a large bowl. Add the chickpeas and mash with a fork or a potato masker. The mixture will not be smooth but a little bit chunky. You may do this in a food processor, but just don't make it smooth. Add the remaining ingredients to the cauliflower mixture and mix well.

Spoon the mixture into the prepared mini muffin cups, pressing the mixture down firmly so that the ingredients stick together. Bake for 30 to 35 minutes. Let the muffins cool in the pan so that they will stay together when removed.

Serve with warm pizza sauce for dunking.

2 tablespoons coconut oil

1 head cauliflower
(3 to 4 cups florets)

1 (15-ounce) can chickpeas, drained
and rinsed

Vegan substitute for 1 egg, prepared

½ cup fresh vegan bread crumbs

⅓ cup grated nondairy mozzarella
cheese

1 teaspoon of your favorite hot
sauce

1 teaspoon dried oregano

1 teaspoon dried parsley

½ teaspoon garlic powder

½ teaspoon onion powder

1 teaspoon sea salt

...Parsley...

Storing in the refrigerator:

Will keep in a tightly sealed container in the refrigerator for 3 to 4 days. You can serve at room temperature or slightly heated.

Freezing:

Freeze in a hard-sided freezer container for 1 to 2 months. To defrost, put in your refrigerator overnight.

Reheating:

To serve, heat on a baking sheet in a 350°F oven for 5 minutes. The muffins do not need to be hot. Alternatively, you can microwave 10 at a time on a microwave-safe dinner plate, on high power for about 15 seconds. Great at room temperature.

Chickpea Balls in Marinara Sauce

This is a good basic hors d'oeuvre ball to have in your repertoire. It holds together well and can be served with a variety of sauces. This recipe calls for a red sauce, and marinara sauce is always a great option for pleasing a crowd.

YIELD: 48 CHICKPEA BALLS | **ACTIVE TIME:** 30 MINUTES | **COOK TIME:** 30 MINUTES | **TOTAL TIME:** 1 HOUR

Preheat the oven to 350°F. Lightly grease a baking sheet with coconut oil.

Heat the coconut oil in a medium-size skillet over medium-high heat. Add the onion and sauté for about 10 minutes. Place in a food processor along with the chickpeas, flour, salt, and pepper. Pulse until combined but still chunky. Do not turn it into a puree.

Roll into 48 balls and place on the prepared baking sheet. Bake for 30 minutes, turning once halfway through.

Serve with the hot marinara sauce.

1 tablespoon coconut oil, plus more for baking sheet

¼ cup white onion, diced small

2 (15-ounce) cans chickpeas, drained and rinsed

½ cup whole wheat flour

2 teaspoons sea salt

¼ teaspoon freshly ground black pepper

Slow Cooker Marinara Sauce (page 231)

Storing in the refrigerator:

Will keep in the refrigerator for 4 to 5 days.

Freezing:

Freeze in a hard-sided freezer container for up to 4 months. This will better protect the balls. To defrost, put in your refrigerator overnight.

Reheating:

To serve, heat on a baking sheet in a 350°F oven for 15 minutes. Lightly toss with heated marinara sauce and serve with toothpicks.

Lentil Balls in Sweet-and-Sour Sauce

There are so many tasty ingredients wrapped up in these little balls. You may find yourself eating them without a sauce and that's okay, too.

YIELD: 48 LENTIL BALLS | **ACTIVE TIME:** 40 MINUTES | **COOK TIME:** 40 MINUTES | **TOTAL TIME:** 1 HOUR 20 MINUTES

Preheat the oven to 350°F. Lightly grease a baking sheet with coconut oil and set aside.

Pick through the lentils to make sure there are no pebbles. Rinse. Bring the 2 cups of water to a boil in a medium-size saucepan. Add the lentils. Bring back to a boil and cook until al dente, about 10 minutes. Drain the lentils when done.

Place the coconut oil in a large skillet and heat over medium-high heat. Add the onion and bell pepper and cook for 5 minutes. Add the grated carrot and cook for another 5 minutes.

Place the mushrooms in a food processor and pulse a couple of times until coarsely chopped. Add the cooked lentils and pulse again until chopped a little bit more but still coarse. Add this mixture to the vegetables in the skillet. Add the garlic powder and cook for 4 minutes. Add the wine and cook for 1 more minute. Add the vegetable stock, bread crumbs, Italian seasoning, salt, and pepper. Stir and let cool so that you can handle the mixture with your hands.

Roll the mixture into 48 balls and place on the prepared baking sheet. Bake for 40 minutes.

Remove from the oven. You can refrigerate or freeze the balls at this point. If serving, toss lightly with sweet-and-sour sauce. Serve with toothpicks.

1 tablespoon coconut oil, plus more for baking sheet

1 cup dried lentils

2 cups water

¼ cup white onion, finely diced

¼ cup red bell pepper, finely diced

1 carrot, grated (about ½ cup)

8 ounces button mushrooms, wiped clean with a clean, damp cloth

½ teaspoon garlic powder

¼ cup dry white wine, such as chardonnay

½ cup vegan vegetable stock

¾ cup vegan bread crumbs

2 tablespoons Italian seasoning

1 teaspoon salt

¼ teaspoon freshly ground black pepper

1 cup of your favorite sweet-and-sour sauce

Storing in the refrigerator:

Will keep in the refrigerator for 4 to 5 days.

Freezing:

Freeze in a hard-sided freezer container for up to 4 months. This will better protect the balls. To defrost, put in your refrigerator overnight.

Reheating:

To serve, heat on a baking sheet in a 350°F oven for 15 minutes. Lightly toss with heated sweet and sour sauce and serve with toothpicks.

Roasted Red Bell Pepper and Tomato Crostini

This appetizer starts with fresh toasted Italian slices. Top that off with a juicy and sweet balsamic-infused topping and you have a winning finger food.

YIELD: ABOUT 24 CROSTINI | **ACTIVE TIME:** 25 MINUTES | **COOK TIME:** 20 MINUTES | **TOTAL TIME:** 45 MINUTES

To make the topping: Turn on the broiler. Place a baking sheet on the lower shelf to catch the drippings.

Place the bell peppers on the top shelf under the broiler. With tongs, turn the bell peppers to get all sides blackened. The bell peppers will be almost completely black. This is how the skin comes off. Remove from the broiler. Let cool and then rub off the blackened skin with a damp paper towel, or peel with a paring knife if you are having trouble. Just grab an edge of the skin with the knife and peel off.

Cut the roasted bell peppers into square chunks. Toss in a medium-size bowl and add the remaining ingredients. Toss well and the topping is done. You may store the topping in the refrigerator or freezer at this point.

To make the bread slices: Just before serving, lay out the bread slices on a baking sheet. Lightly brush each slice with the coconut oil. The new silicone brushes are great for this; they wash really easily. Put the baking sheet under the broiler. Don't do anything else. Just stand there and keep checking the bread and don't let it burn. It only takes a couple of minutes. After the toasts are lightly browned, remove from the broiler. You can keep them in the refrigerator for later use, too, such as if you are serving the crostini tomorrow or in a few days.

FOR THE TOPPING:

3 red bell peppers

3 Roma tomatoes, chopped

1 clove garlic, finely diced

2 tablespoons balsamic vinegar

1 tablespoon coconut oil

1 teaspoon dried basil, or
  1 tablespoon fresh

1 teaspoon salt

¼ teaspoon freshly ground black
  pepper

FOR THE BREAD SLICES:

1 long loaf vegan Italian bread,
  sliced

3 tablespoons coconut oil

Storing in the refrigerator:

The topping and toasts will keep in the refrigerator for 4 to 5 days. Keep them separated. To serve, toss the topping and spoon onto the toasts.

Freezing:

You may freeze the topping in a hard-sided freezer container for up to 4 months. To defrost, put in your refrigerator overnight. Before serving, toss and spoon onto the toasts.

Roasted Artichoke and Hearts of Palm Spread

This is a nice versatile spread. It can be used as a dip with vegetables and chips, spread on mini toasts, and stuffed in a variety of vegetables, such as mini bell peppers. All are good appetizers in their own right. Use it in wraps and on sandwiches, too.

YIELD: 3 CUPS SPREAD | **ACTIVE TIME:** 10 MINUTES | **COOK TIME:** 15 MINUTES | **TOTAL TIME:** 25 MINUTES

Preheat the oven to 425°F.

Cut any tough edges off the leaves from the artichoke hearts. Cut the hearts of palm in half. Place the coconut oil in a medium-size bowl. Add the artichoke hearts, hearts of palm, and garlic. Toss and pour out onto a baking sheet. Roast for 15 minutes, or until you can easily pierce the garlic with a fork. Remove from the oven and place the vegetables in a food processor. Process until almost smooth or smooth, your choice. If you would like the mixture a bit thinner, you can add a tablespoon of olive oil. The spread is ready to serve with small toasts and pretzels. Sturdier vegetables such as carrots would be wonderful, too.

1 (14-ounce) can artichoke hearts, drained

1 (14-ounce) can hearts of palm, drained

2 tablespoons coconut oil

6 cloves garlic, peeled

½ teaspoon sea salt

¼ teaspoon freshly ground black pepper

1 tablespoon olive oil (optional)

Storing in the refrigerator:

Will keep in the refrigerator for 4 to 5 days. Serve it chilled, at room temperature, or warmed.

Freezing:

You can freeze the spread in a hard-sided freezer container for up to 4 months. To defrost, put in your refrigerator overnight. Serve it chilled, at room temperature, or warmed.

Spinach Artichoke Dip

Spinach and artichoke are such a wonderful combination that the pairing is becoming a classic. Serve with an assortment of whole-grain crackers or pita bread wedges. Equally good served with a tray of raw vegetables, such as broccoli, mushrooms, carrots, and celery sticks.

YIELD: 3½ CUPS DIP | **ACTIVE TIME:** 15 MINUTES | **COOK TIME:** 0 | **TOTAL TIME:** 15 MINUTES

Place the baby spinach in a food processor and pulse a few times to roughly chop. Remove from the processor and set aside.

Cut any tough edges off the leaves from the artichoke hearts. Put in the food processor and process to chop very small but not smooth. Remove from the processor and pick out any noticeably fibrous parts. Set aside.

Add the chickpeas, garlic, tahini, lemon juice, salt, ground pepper, cayenne, and olive oil to the food processor. Process until blended very well but not completely smooth. Add the chopped artichokes and spinach and process again until well blended. Taste for seasonings.

4 ounces baby spinach

1 (14-ounce) can artichoke hearts, drained and rinsed

1 (15-ounce) can chickpeas, drained and rinsed

1 clove garlic

2 tablespoons tahini

2 tablespoons fresh lemon juice

½ teaspoon sea salt

¼ teaspoon freshly ground black pepper

¼ teaspoon cayenne pepper

¼ cup olive oil

NOTE:

You can use coconut oil, but it gets very hard if you are storing it in the refrigerator and it takes quite a long time to soften. For these reasons I prefer olive oil for this recipe.

Storing in the refrigerator:

Will keep in the refrigerator for 4 for 5 days. Serve it chilled, at room temperature, or warmed.

Freezing:

Freeze in a hard-sided freezer container for up to 4 months. To defrost, put in your refrigerator overnight. Serve it chilled, at room temperature, or warmed.

Roasted Red Bell Pepper Hummus

This is a robust dip that can be dressed up for a cocktail party or roughed up for game day. Everybody wants a scoop.

YIELD: 2½ CUPS HUMMUS (SEE NOTE) | **ACTIVE TIME:** 10 MINUTES | **COOK TIME:** 10 MINUTES |
TOTAL TIME: 20 MINUTES

First, roast the red bell pepper. Heat the broiler. Place a baking sheet on the lower shelf to catch any drippings.

With tongs, place the bell pepper on the top shelf under the broiler. With tongs, turn the bell pepper often to get all sides blackened. When the bell pepper is black, take it out of the broiler. Let cool and then rub off the blackened skin with a damp paper towel, or peel with a paring knife if you are having trouble. Just grab an edge of the skin with the knife and peel off.

Now, just put everything into a food processor and blend well. No need to pregrind anything; it all blends together perfectly. Turn off the processor and scrape the sides a couple of times during processing.

Serve with chips and vegetables.

1 (15-ounce) can chickpeas, drained and rinsed

1 red bell pepper, or a (4-ounce) jar roasted red bell peppers

1 tablespoon tahini, or cashew or almond butter (see note)

Juice of 1 lemon (3 to 4 tablespoons juice)

1 tablespoon coconut oil

½ teaspoon ground cumin

½ teaspoon salt

¼ teaspoon freshly ground black pepper

NOTES:

This recipe is simple to double or triple, so buy your ingredients according to how much dip you will need.

I have used either tahini, cashew butter, or almond butter at one time or another, and I don't want you to go out and buy tahini for one tablespoon.

Storing in the refrigerator:

Will keep in the refrigerator for 4 to 5 days. Serve it chilled, at room temperature, or warmed.

Freezing:

Freeze the dip in a hard-sided freezer container for up to 4 months. To defrost, put in your refrigerator overnight. Serve it chilled, at room temperature, or warmed.

Edamame Hummus

Here is a clean-tasting and flavorful dip with just a hint of heat. It will be the modernized bean dip that you have been wanting.

YIELD: 3½ CUPS HUMMUS | **ACTIVE TIME:** 10 MINUTES | **COOK TIME:** 10 HOURS | **TOTAL TIME:** 20 MINUTES

Cook the edamame according to the package directions. Set aside to cool.

In a food processor, combine the jalapeño and garlic and pulse until finely chopped. Add the cooled edamame and chickpeas. Process until almost smooth.

Add the remaining ingredients and pulse until well blended. If the mixture seems too thick, you may add 1 tablespoon of water at a time, up to ¼ cup, blending between additions.

Taste for seasoning and add more salt, if needed.

1 (10- to 16-ounce) bag frozen shelled edamame

1 (15-ounce) can chickpeas, drained and rinsed

2 tablespoons tahini

¼ cup fresh lime juice

1 small jalapeño chile, seeded and finely diced

1 clove garlic, cleaned

¼ cup fresh cilantro

1 teaspoon sea salt

¼ cup plus 1 tablespoon olive oil

Storing in the refrigerator:

Will keep in the refrigerator for 4 to 5 days. Serve it chilled, at room temperature, or warmed.

Freezing:

Freeze the dip in a hard-sided freezer container for up to 4 months. To defrost, put in your refrigerator overnight. Serve it chilled, at room temperature, or warmed.

Apple Pie Crescent Triangles

Here is a simple crescent recipe that is not only a great appetizer choice, but can also work as a snack or dessert. Make as many as you want for a party, but make extra for your home.

YIELD: 16 PIE TRIANGLES | **ACTIVE TIME:** 30 MINUTES | **COOK TIME:** 15 MINUTES | **TOTAL TIME:** 45 MINUTES

2 teaspoons ground cinnamon

¼ cup coconut sugar

¼ cup granulated sugar

2 cans vegan refrigerated crescent rolls (see note)

2 Granny Smith apples

1 cup walnuts, chopped

Preheat the oven to 375°F. For ease of cleaning, place a silicone baking mat or parchment paper on two baking sheets. Set aside.

Mix the cinnamon and sugars and set aside.

Open a can of crescent rolls and roll out the sheet. There are eight divisions that are shaped as triangles. Separate them and place the short, fat end closest to you so that you can roll away from you.

Cut one apple in half, along the core, and then in half again. You will have four sections. Peel and core each piece. Cut those in half also so you have eight crescent-shaped pieces of apple.

Dip a piece of apple in the cinnamon-sugar and cover liberally. Lay crosswise with the end of the crescent dough. Sprinkle with a few walnut pieces and roll up. Place on a baking sheet with the tip of the dough on the underside. Continue with the rest of the apple.

Bake in the center of the oven for 12 to 15 minutes, until a nice golden color. The bottoms will be darker, so be careful. Only do one pan at a time, to obtain a more even color. Remove from the oven and let cool for at least 10 minutes. While they are still warm, sprinkle with the cinnamon/sugar mixture.

I like to work with one apple at a time because they turn brown so quickly. They will still be white with this process. Open the other can of crescent dough and repeat the process.

NOTE:
Use low-fat crescent rolls, to avoid trans fats.

Storing in the refrigerator:

The apple pie triangles will keep in the refrigerator for 4 to 5 days.

Freezing:

You can store the triangles in a hard-sided freezer container. This will better protect them. To defrost, put in your refrigerator overnight.

Reheating:

To serve, heat on a baking sheet in a 350°F oven for 10 minutes.

Soft Cinnamon-Sugar Pretzel Bites

Who doesn't like soft pretzels? For a party, the way to go is to make them into bite-size balls. After baking, roll them in cinnamon-sugar and they are done.

YIELD: ABOUT 60 PRETZELS | **ACTIVE TIME:** 1 HOUR | **COOK TIME:** 12 MINUTES | **TOTAL TIME:** 1 HOUR 12 MINUTES

Lightly grease a baking sheet with coconut oil.

To make the pretzels: Add the yeast to the warm water and stir. Set aside for about 5 minutes.

In a large bowl, combine the flours, baking soda, brown sugar, and salt. Mix together. Add the coconut oil and the yeast mixture. Mix well. Turn out onto a lightly floured surface and knead until smooth and elastic, 8 to 10 minutes. Divide the dough into fourths and roll each into a cigar shape 15 to 17 inches long. Cut each length into 1-inch pieces. Place the pieces on the prepared baking sheet so that they do not touch. Let rest for 10 minutes.

Preheat the oven to 350°F while the pretzel pieces are resting and then bake for 10 to 12 minutes. Test a piece and see whether the dough is done on the inside. When done, remove from the oven and let cool on the baking sheet.

To make the coating: Mix the granulated sugar and cinnamon together and place in a resealable plastic bag for tossing. Put the melted nondairy butter in a medium-size to large bowl and toss in all the pretzels. Stir so that all of the balls are evenly coated with melted nondairy butter on all sides. Now, transfer a few of the bites (about half) to the bag of the cinnamon-sugar. Seal the bag and toss so that all the pretzels are evenly coated. Take out the pretzels and place in a bowl. Put the remaining pretzel bites in the bag and repeat the process.

FOR THE PRETZELS:

1 tablespoon coconut oil, plus more for baking sheet

1 cup warm water (110°F)

1 (¼-ounce) packet active dry yeast

1¼ cups all-purpose flour, plus more for dusting

¾ cup whole wheat flour

1 teaspoon baking soda

2 teaspoons light brown sugar

½ teaspoon salt

FOR THE COATING:

½ cup granulated sugar

1 tablespoon ground cinnamon

½ cup (1 stick, 4 ounces) nondairy butter, melted

Storing:

The pretzels will keep in an airtight container at room temperature for 2 to 3 days. If they are not kept in an airtight container, they can become hard.

Freezing:

You can freeze the pretzels for about a month. They will become a bit harder.

To soften after storage:

Hardened pretzels can be softened by a microwaving on medium power for 5 to 10 seconds. Toss again in a fresh batch of cinnamon-sugar.

Cinnamon Crescent Rings

It is amazing how fancy some recipes can appear when there is hardly any work. These cinnamon crescent rings are tempting to save for the holidays but go ahead and indulge once in a while.

YIELD: 4 CRESCENT RINGS | **ACTIVE TIME:** 20 MINUTES | **COOK TIME:** 15 MINUTES | **TOTAL TIME:** 35 MINUTES

To make the rings: Preheat the oven to 375°F.

Mix the walnuts, nondairy milk, vanilla, sugar, cinnamon, and maple syrup in a small saucepan.

Heat over medium heat, stirring, for about 2 minutes to melt the sugar and blend all ingredients. Set aside and let cool.

Open one can of crescent rolls and lay out on a lightly floured surface.

Press the seams together and press out with your fingers, or a rolling pin, to 14 x 8-inch rectangle.

Spread the cooled walnut mixture evenly over the whole surface.

Unroll the other can of crescent rolls onto a piece of waxed paper.

Seal the perforations and press out with your fingers, or a rolling pin, to a 14 x 8-inch rectangle.

Pick up the waxed paper carefully and invert it over the walnut filling lining up the edges of the dough. Remove the waxed paper carefully. Press and seal all the edges.

Working along the long side, cut crosswise into eight 8-inch-long strips. Twist each strip and bring around the ends to seal into a circle. Lay on an ungreased baking sheet.

Bake for 12 to 15 minutes, until light golden brown.

To make the glaze: While the rolls bake, combine the maple syrup and nondairy butter in a small saucepan. Heat through over low heat.

When the rings come out of the oven, brush each generously with the glaze. Serve hot.

FOR THE RINGS:

1½ cups walnuts, finely chopped

¼ cup nondairy milk

½ teaspoon vanilla extract

2 tablespoons granulated sugar

½ teaspoon ground cinnamon

2 tablespoons pure maple syrup

2 (8-ounce) cans vegan crescent rolls

All-purpose flour, for dusting

FOR THE GLAZE:

2 tablespoons pure maple syrup

1 tablespoon nondairy butter

Storing in the refrigerator:

Will keep covered in the refrigerator for about 1 week.

Freezing:

Freeze in either resealable plastic bags or a hard-sided freezer container for up to 3 months. Defrost in the refrigerator.

Chocolate Layered Cinnamon Rolls

Cinnamon rolls are delicious treats, but if you have chocolate cravings, enjoy these delectable treats that are over and beyond.

YIELD: 9 LARGE ROLLS | **ACTIVE TIME:** 1½ HOURS | **COOK TIME:** 25 MINUTES | **TOTAL TIME:** 1 HOUR 55 MINUTES

Heat the water, nondairy milk, and 2 tablespoons of the nondairy butter in a microwave on high power for a few seconds, until warm (110°F). Add the yeast, stir, and set aside for about 10 minutes.

In a bowl, stir together the flour, baking powder, and salt. Set aside.

Stir the maple syrup into the yeast mixture. Pour into a large bowl. Beating by hand or using an electric mixer on medium speed, add 1 cup of the flour mixture to the yeast mixture. Continue, adding the flour mixture, 1 cup at a time, until all the flour is incorporated. If working by hand, turn the dough out onto a floured surface and knead for about a minute. If using a mixer, switch to the dough hook and mix until the dough forms a ball. The dough will be a little sticky.

Pat a little oil all over the ball of dough and place back in the bowl. Cover the bowl with a clean towel and place in a warm place to rise for 1 hour.

Butter an 8-inch square baking pan.

Mix the cinnamon and sugar together and set aside.

Turn out the dough onto a lightly floured surface and roll out to a 10 x 16-inch rectangle.

Melt the remaining 2 tablespoons of nondairy butter. Brush 1 tablespoon of the nondairy butter all over the surface. Sprinkle with the cinnamon-sugar. Sprinkle with the chocolate chips.

¼ cup water

¾ cup nondairy milk

4 tablespoons nondairy butter, divided, plus more for pan

2¼ teaspoons active dry yeast

3 cups all-purpose flour, plus more for dusting

1 teaspoon baking powder

⅔ teaspoon sea salt

1 tablespoon pure maple syrup

1 tablespoon coconut oil, for rolling dough

5 tablespoons sugar

2 teaspoons ground cinnamon

½ cup vegan chocolate chips

FOR THE TOPPING:

¼ cup nondairy milk

⅓ cup vegan chocolate chips

1 teaspoon vanilla extract

Starting at the short end, roll up the dough. Cut into nine slices 1½ to 2 inches wide. Place the rolls in three rows of three, seam side down, in the prepared pan. Brush with the remaining tablespoon of melted nondairy butter. Cover with a clean towel and set in a warm place to rise for 30 minutes.

While the rolls rise, preheat the oven to 350°F.

Uncover the pan and bake for 25 to 30 minutes. Let cool.

To make the topping: Microwave the nondairy milk and chocolate chips together on medium power for 15 seconds. Stir and keep heating at 5-second increments until completely melted. Chocolate will burn in the microwave if you don't watch it carefully. When melted, stir in the vanilla. Drizzle, back and forth, all over the top of the baked rolls. These are ready to eat anytime.

Storing in the refrigerator:

Will keep covered in the refrigerator for up to 4 days.

Freezing:

Freeze in airtight containers for up to 3 months. Let defrost in the refrigerator overnight and they are ready to eat.

Trail Mix Donuts

There is just something fun about donuts. These donuts aren't too sweet and they even have an extra crunch for satisfaction. Baked, not fried, they travel well.

YIELD: 12 DONUTS | **ACTIVE TIME:** 15 MINUTES | **COOK TIME:** 16 MINUTES | **TOTAL TIME:** 31 MINUTES

Preheat the oven to 350°F. Lightly grease donut pans with coconut oil for a total of 12 donuts, or use silicone donut pans.

In a large bowl, combine the flour, sugar, baking powder, salt, and cinnamon.

In a medium-size bowl, combine the coconut oil, nondairy milk, egg substitute, and vanilla. Mix well.

Add the dry ingredients to the wet ingredients and mix until just combined.

Evenly distribute the batter in the prepared pans.

Bake for 14 to 16 minutes.

When done, pop the donuts out of the pans and let cool on a wire rack. These are great warm or cold.

⅔ cup coconut oil, plus more for pan

1¼ cups whole wheat flour

¾ cup sugar

½ teaspoon baking powder

½ teaspoon sea salt

½ teaspoon salt

½ teaspoon ground cinnamon

½ cup nondairy milk

Vegan substitute for 1 egg, prepared

1 teaspoon vanilla extract

¾ cup trail mix of your choice

Storing in the refrigerator:

Will keep covered in the refrigerator for about 1 week.

Freezing:

Freeze in either resealable plastic bags or a hard-sided freezer container for up to 3 months. Defrost in the refrigerator.

Irresistible Granola

Granola can be good in so many different ways. The experimentation seems endless, but here is one recipe that I think has all of the most desirable flavors, fragrance, and nutrition rolled up in one big batch.

YIELD: 14 CUPS GRANOLA | **ACTIVE TIME:** 15 MINUTES | **COOK TIME:** 20 MINUTES | **TOTAL TIME:** 35 MINUTES

Preheat the oven to 325°F.

In a microwavable bowl, heat the maple syrup and coconut oil together for 2½ minutes.

In a large bowl, combine the remaining ingredients, except the raisins and cranberries. Add the maple syrup mixture. Stir well.

Spread out on a large baking pan. Bake for 20 minutes. Remove from the oven and add the raisins and cranberries. Mix well. Let cool. When completely cool, pack in airtight containers. I use quart-size canning jars.

¾ cup pure maple syrup

½ cup coconut oil

5 cups rolled oats

1 cup pecans, coarsely chopped

1 cup blanched slivered almonds

1 cup walnuts, coarsely chopped

½ cup pepitas

½ cup sprouted pumpkin seeds

2 cups unsweetened shredded coconut

½ cup hull-less sunflower seeds

⅔ cup raisins

⅔ cup dried cranberries

Storing in the refrigerator:

Will keep in airtight containers for up to 3 months.

Freezing:

Freeze in airtight containers for up to 1 year.

Fruit-Filled Half-Moon Pies

When you don't have much time and you don't want to bake a big pie, go ahead and make one of these simple fold-over half-pies. No pie pan necessary.

YIELD: 8 SERVINGS | **ACTIVE TIME:** 20 MINUTES | **COOK TIME:** 35 MINUTES | **TOTAL TIME:** 55 MINUTES

Preheat the oven to 375°F. You will need two baking sheets.

In a medium-size saucepan, combine the apple, coconut sugar, 1 tablespoon of the water, and the lemon juice. Cook over medium heat until bubbly. Cover, lower the heat to low, and cook for 6 to 8 minutes, stirring every couple of minutes to make sure the mixture is not sticking.

Take the piecrusts out of their pouch and lay on a baking sheet. Let them come to room temperature so that you can unfold it more easily without the dough tearing.

In a small bowl, mix the flour, granulated sugar, and salt. Stir into the bubbling apple mixture until the mixture thickens. This will take about a minute. Remove from the heat and stir in the nondairy butter and vanilla. Add the frozen blueberries and fold into the hot mixture. Let cool for about 10 minutes. The mixture will become blueberry color.

Unfold one of the piecrusts on the baking sheet. Set the other aside on the second baking sheet. Spoon half of the cooled fruit filling onto the center of the unfolded crust. Carefully fold over the piecrust to meet the other edge so that you have a half-moon shape. Press the edge together, roll the edge by over one turn all around the open edge, and then press the rolled edge with fork tines for even a better seal. Cut a few small slits on the top of the piecrust. Repeat this process with the other piecrust and remaining filling, on the other baking sheet.

Bake for 25 to 35 minutes, until the crust is golden brown. Switch the positions of the baking sheets about 15 minutes into baking. Remove from the oven when golden brown and let cool on the baking sheets. Use a metal spatula to loosen the pies from the baking sheets and cut each half-moon pie into fourths.

1 Granny Smith apple, cored and thinly sliced

¼ cup coconut sugar

2 tablespoons water, divided

1 teaspoon fresh lemon juice

1 tablespoon all-purpose flour

1 tablespoon granulated sugar

¼ teaspoon salt

1 tablespoon nondairy butter

½ teaspoon vanilla extract

¾ cup frozen blueberries

Storing in the refrigerator:

Will keep covered in the refrigerator for up to 4 days.

Freezing:

Freeze in airtight containers for up to 3 months. Let defrost in the refrigerator overnight and they are ready to serve.

Orange Pecan Muffins

These muffins are a meal in themselves. They're packed full of fiber, nuts, and citrus flavor. The drizzle isn't necessary over the top. It just makes them a little prettier.

YIELD: 10 MUFFINS | **ACTIVE TIME:** 20 MINUTES | **COOK TIME:** 20 MINUTES | **TOTAL TIME:** 40 MINUTES

Preheat the oven to 400°F. Place muffin liners in 10 muffin cups.

In a medium-size bowl, combine the flour, cereal, coconut sugar, baking powder, and salt. Mix well. Pour in the coconut oil and mix well. Add the egg substitute, orange juice, and nondairy milk. Stir well. Fold in the pecans.

Divide the batter among the prepared muffin cups. Bake for 20 minutes.

Let cool for 10 minutes and then transfer to a wire rack to cool completely.

To make the drizzle: Mix the orange juice and powdered sugar together. If it does not seem thin enough, you can add water, ½ teaspoon at a time. Drizzle right onto the center of each muffin and allow it to go over the sides.

1½ cups all-purpose flour

½ cup vegan bran cereal, processed to crumbs

¼ cup coconut sugar

1½ teaspoons baking powder

½ teaspoon sea salt

¼ cup coconut oil

Vegan substitute for 1 egg, prepared

¼ cup fresh orange juice

½ cup nondairy milk

¾ cup pecans, chopped

FOR THE DRIZZLE:

Juice of 1 orange

¼ cup powdered sugar

Storing in the refrigerator:

Will keep covered in the refrigerator for up to 4 days.

Freezing:

Freeze in airtight containers for up to 3 months. Let defrost in the refrigerator overnight and they are ready to serve.

Energy Date Muffins

It's always good to have a breakfast you can grab as you are going out the door. These are perfect and you can actually enjoy them right out of the freezer because they defrost so quickly.

YIELD: 12 MUFFINS | **ACTIVE TIME:** 20 MINUTES | **COOK TIME:** 15 MINUTES | **TOTAL TIME:** 35 MINUTES

Preheat the oven to 400°F. Place muffin liners in 12 muffin cups.

In a large bowl, combine the flour, oats, sugars, baking powder, baking soda, and salt. In a medium-size bowl, stir together the yogurt, nondairy milk, coconut oil, vanilla, and egg substitute. Add the yogurt mixture to the flour mixture. Mix until just combined. Fold in the dates.

Fill each prepared muffin cup about halfway full. Bake for 15 minutes. Let cool for about 10 minutes and then transfer to wire racks to cool completely.

NOTE:
You can chop your dates, but they are too sticky to put in a food processor. One way that I handle dates is to cut them with kitchen scissors.

1¼ cups whole wheat flour

⅓ cup quick cooking oats

¼ cup flaxseed meal

¼ cup granulated sugar

¼ cup light brown sugar

1 teaspoon baking powder

1 teaspoon baking soda

¼ teaspoon salt

1 cup soy yogurt

¼ cup nondairy milk

2 tablespoons coconut oil

1 teaspoon vanilla extract

Vegan substitute for 1 egg, prepared

1½ cups dates, chopped (see note)

Storing in the refrigerator:
Will keep covered in the refrigerator for up to 1 week.

Freezing:
Freeze in either resealable plastic bags or a hard-sided freezer container for up to 3 months.

Good Morning Muffins

As the name implies, these pretty muffins will help you start your morning. There is fruit, vegetable, and nuts inside to provide the nourishment that you need.

YIELD: 12 MUFFINS | **ACTIVE TIME:** 20 MINUTES | **COOK TIME:** 15 MINUTES | **TOTAL TIME:** 35 MINUTES

Preheat the oven to 350°F. Place muffin liners in 12 muffin cups.

In a large bowl, combine the flours, sugars, cinnamon, baking powder, baking soda, and salt. In a medium-size bowl, stir together the egg substitute, coconut oil, and vanilla. Add to the flour mixture. Mix until just combined. Fold in the apple, dates, carrot, and pecans. Mix until just combined.

Divide the batter evenly among the prepared muffin cups. Bake for 25 to 30 minutes. Let cool for about 10 minutes and then transfer to wire racks to cool completely.

1 cup whole wheat flour

⅓ cup all-purpose flour

½ cup coconut sugar

¼ cup light brown sugar

1 teaspoon ground cinnamon

1 teaspoon baking powder

½ teaspoon baking soda

¼ teaspoon sea salt

Vegan substitute for 2 eggs, prepared

⅔ cup coconut oil

1 teaspoon vanilla extract

1 apple, cored, peeled, and diced

½ cup dates, diced

1 carrot, grated (½ cup)

½ cup pecans, chopped

Storing in the refrigerator:

Will keep covered in the refrigerator for up to 1 week.

Freezing:

Freeze in either resealable plastic bags or a hard-sided freezer container for up to 3 months.

Crunchy-Topped Coffee Cake

The perfect brunch cake that you can have ready in no time at all. The topping bakes up to a softly crisp and bumpy layer that makes this cake deliciously unique.

YIELD: 12 CAKE SQUARES | **ACTIVE TIME:** 25 MINUTES | **COOK TIME:** 30 MINUTES | **TOTAL TIME:** 55 MINUTES

Preheat the oven to 350°F. Lightly oil a 9 x 13-inch baking pan.

To make the cake base: In a large bowl, combine the flours, sugar, baking powder, and salt. Cut in the nondairy butter until the mixture resembles a coarse meal. Add the egg substitute, nondairy milk, and vanilla. Mix until just combined. Pour into the prepared baking pan and spread out evenly.

To make the streusel: In a medium-size bowl, combine the flour, sugar, and cinnamon. Mix in the melted nondairy butter. It will be a moist mixture. Dot the streusel around on top of the batter until it is as evenly disbursed as you can get it.

Bake for 25 to 30 minutes, or until a toothpick inserted into the center comes out clean. Let cool and cut in the pan.

FOR THE CAKE BASE:

1 cup all-purpose flour

1 cup whole wheat pastry flour

¾ cup granulated sugar

2 teaspoons baking powder

½ teaspoon salt

½ cup (1 stick, 4 ounces) nondairy butter

Vegan substitute for 1 egg, prepared

½ cup nondairy milk

1½ teaspoons vanilla extract

FOR THE STREUSEL TOPPING:

¼ cup all-purpose flour

⅔ cup granulated sugar

1 teaspoon ground cinnamon

4 tablespoons nondairy butter, melted

Storing in the refrigerator:

Will keep covered in the refrigerator for up to 1 week.

Freezing:

Freeze in either resealable plastic bags or a hard-sided freezer container for up to 3 months.

German Apple Coffee Cake

This sweet and fruity coffee cake is perfect for a holiday brunch spread. It is deceptively easy and obviously special.

YIELD: 8 SERVINGS | **ACTIVE TIME:** 20 MINUTES | **COOK TIME:** 25 MINUTES | **TOTAL TIME:** 45 MINUTES

Preheat the oven to 400°F. Lightly grease a 9-inch springform pan with coconut oil.

In a medium-size bowl, mix the flours, turbinado sugar, baking powder, and salt.

In a large bowl, stir together the egg substitute, nondairy milk, banana, and coconut oil.

Stir the dry ingredients into the wet ingredients until just moistened. Fold in the grated apple.

Pour into the prepared springform pan.

To make the topping: Mix the topping ingredients and sprinkle all over the top of the batter.

Bake for 25 minutes, or until a toothpick inserted into the center comes out clean. Let cool in the pan on a wire rack for 10 minutes. Remove the sides of the pan.

3 tablespoons coconut oil, plus more for pan

1 cup all-purpose flour

1 cup whole wheat flour

½ cup turbinado sugar

1½ teaspoons baking powder

½ teaspoon salt

Vegan substitute for 1 egg, prepared

½ cup nondairy milk

½ banana, mashed

1 apple, cored, peeled, and grated (¾ to 1 cup)

FOR THE TOPPING:

1 tablespoon all-purpose flour

1 tablespoon turbinado sugar

¼ teaspoon ground cinnamon

2 tablespoons chopped walnuts

Storing in the refrigerator:
Will keep covered in the refrigerator for up to 1 week.

Freezing:
Freeze in either resealable plastic bags or a hard-sided freezer container for up to 3 months.

Coconut Cream Cinnamon Coffee Cake

One of the perks to this light and moist coffee cake is that it keeps a long time in the fridge. No fussing; just enjoy a piece when you have the hankering.

YIELD: 16 SQUARES | **ACTIVE TIME:** 15 MINUTES | **COOK TIME:** 25 MINUTES | **TOTAL TIME:** 40 MINUTES

Preheat the oven to 375°F. Lightly grease a 9-inch square pan with coconut oil and lightly flour.

In a large bowl, combine the flour, baking powder, salt, and turbinado sugar. Stir in the egg substitute, coconut oil, and coconut cream. Mix until just combined.

Spread evenly in the prepared pan.

To make the topping: Combine all the topping ingredients. Sprinkle evenly over the batter.

Bake for 20 to 25 minutes, or until a toothpick inserted into the center comes out clean. Let cool in the pan on a wire rack for 10 minutes. Transfer to a wire rack and cut into squares to serve.

¼ cup coconut oil, plus more for pan

1½ cups all-purpose flour, plus more for pan

2 teaspoons baking powder

½ teaspoon salt

½ cup turbinado sugar

Vegan substitute for 1 egg, prepared

¾ cup full-fat coconut cream (17% to 22% fat)

FOR THE TOPPING:

⅓ cup all-purpose flour

½ cup granulated sugar

¾ teaspoon ground cinnamon

4 tablespoons nondairy butter, at room temperature

Storing in the refrigerator:

Will keep covered in the refrigerator for up to 1 week.

Freezing:

Freeze in either resealable plastic bags or a hard-sided freezer container for up to 3 months.

Historical Raisin Bread

Originally this bread was called War Cake, the reason being that during WWII many foods were rationed and dairy products were among them. Now we choose not to have butter, milk, and eggs, so this recipe comes in very handy. I have updated very few of the ingredients.

YIELD: 1 LOAF | **ACTIVE TIME:** 15 MINUTES | **COOK TIME:** 45 MINUTES | **TOTAL TIME:** 1 HOUR

In a medium-size saucepan, combine both varieties of raisins, and the coconut oil, brown sugar, cloves, cinnamon, nutmeg, and water. Bring to a boil, then turn down the heat and simmer for 10 minutes.

Let cool to room temperature, about 1½ hours.

Preheat the oven to 350°F. Lightly grease a 9 x 5-inch loaf pan with coconut oil.

In a large bowl, stir together the flour, baking powder, and salt. Add the cooled raisin mixture and blend well.

Pour into the prepared loaf pan and bake for 45 minutes.

Let cool in the pan for 10 minutes and then turn out onto a wire rack to cool completely.

Slice and serve warm or cold.

1 cup golden raisins

1 cup raisins

1 tablespoon coconut oil, plus more for pan

1 cup light brown sugar

¼ teaspoon ground cloves

1 teaspoon ground cinnamon

1 teaspoon ground nutmeg

1 cup water

2 cups whole wheat flour

1½ teaspoons baking powder

½ teaspoon salt

Storing in the refrigerator:

Will keep covered in the refrigerator for about 1 week.

Freezing:

Freeze in either resealable plastic bags or a hard-sided freezer container for up to 3 months. Defrost in the refrigerator and serve warm or cold.

Reheating:

Unwrap a burrito from its plastic wrap. Place on a microwave-safe plate, let defrost for 4 minutes, then microwave immediately on high power for 15 seconds on one side. Roll the burrito over and cook for 15 seconds on the other side. You can also defrost them in the refrigerator overnight and then microwave as described.

Classic Breakfast Burritos

Classics are just that. They are something that have worn the weather of time and people are still coming back. That is exactly what this burrito stands for. A good classic solid meal.

YIELD: 10 BURRITOS | **ACTIVE TIME:** 15 MINUTES | **COOK TIME:** 30 MINUTES | **TOTAL TIME:** 45 MINUTES

Place the refried beans in a small bowl and mix to incorporate the oils from the can. Add the nutritional yeast and stir well.

Heat the oil in a 10-inch skillet over medium-high heat. Add the bell peppers and sauté for 5 minutes. Add the onion and cook for 10 more minutes. Remove the mixture from the pan. Add the mushrooms and cook for 10 to 15 minutes, or until they shrink by about one-quarter of their size. Remove from the heat.

Now, to assemble the burritos. Lay out your tortillas on a counter. Spread a little less than ¼ cup of the refried bean mixture down the center of each tortilla. Evenly divide the bell pepper mixture down the center of the beans. Distribute the mushrooms evenly over the last layer.

Roll up each tortilla nice and tight. Heat two burritos at a time in the microwave on high power for a little over a minute: 45 seconds on one side, then roll over and switch positions for 30 seconds on the other side.

Serve with salsa on the side.

1 (14.5-ounce) can vegan refried beans

¼ cup nutritional yeast

1 tablespoon coconut oil

1 red bell pepper, diced

1 green bell pepper, diced

1 yellow onion, diced small

16 ounces cremini mushrooms

10 vegan whole wheat tortillas

1 cup of your favorite salsa, for serving

Storing in the refrigerator:

Place the burritos into a large resealable plastic bag and keep in the refrigerator for up to 4 days.

Freezing:

Wrap each burrito individually in plastic wrap so that you can pull out one or two at a time for a quick breakfast. Place the wrapped burritos in one large freezer bag. Freeze for up to 4 months.

Loaded Breakfast Burritos

These burritos have a great combination of multiple ingredients. Fill up your tortilla as fat as you like!

YIELD: 10 BURRITOS | **ACTIVE TIME:** 15 MINUTES | **COOK TIME:** 40 MINUTES | **TOTAL TIME:** 55 MINUTES

Cook the brown rice. If you don't have a rice cooker, place the rice and 2 cups of water in a medium-size saucepan. Bring the rice to a boil over high heat. Cover the pot and let simmer over medium-high heat until the water is absorbed and rice is tender, 40 to 50 minutes. Check that the rice is done and then remove from the heat.

Heat the coconut oil in a 10-inch skillet over medium-high heat. Add the bell pepper, onion, and mushrooms. Sauté until the onion is translucent and the mushrooms have cooked down, about 15 minutes.

Add the cooked rice, vegan sausage, black beans, oregano, coriander, cumin, and chili powder. Cook, stirring, over medium heat for about 5 minutes. Add the salt and pepper and taste. Set aside to cool a bit.

Lay out your tortillas in a couple of rows. This makes the assembly go faster and always helps divvy up the stuffing evenly. Place about ⅓ cup of the mixture in the center of each tortilla. Even up all of the stuffing on all 10 tortillas. On each tortilla, spread the stuffing in a long row from one side of the tortilla to the other. Fold one edge of the tortilla over the filling and roll tightly into a long roll. Heat two burritos at a time in the microwave on high power for little over 1 minute: 45 seconds on one side, then roll over and cook for 30 seconds on the other side.

1 cup uncooked brown rice

1 tablespoon coconut oil

1 red bell pepper, diced

½ red onion, diced

1 (8 ounce) package cremini mushrooms, chopped

1 (10-ounce) package vegan sausage, chopped

1 (15-ounce) can black beans, drained and rinsed

½ teaspoon dried oregano

¼ teaspoon ground coriander

¼ teaspoon ground cumin

¼ teaspoon chili powder

1 teaspoon salt

¼ teaspoon freshly ground black pepper

10 whole wheat flour tortillas

Storing in the refrigerator:

Place the burritos into a large resealable plastic bag and keep in the refrigerator for up to 4 days.

Freezing:

Wrap each burrito individually in plastic wrap so that you can pull out one or two at a time for a quick breakfast. Place the wrapped burritos in one large freezer bag. Freeze for up to 4 months.

Reheating:

Unwrap a burrito from its plastic wrap. Place on a microwave-safe plate, set to defrost for 4 minutes, then microwave immediately on high power for 15 seconds on one side. Roll the burrito over and cook for 15 seconds on the other side. You can also defrost them in the refrigerator overnight and then microwave as described.

Banana Oat Bran Waffles

Here is a breakfast that is so good in so many ways. It has lots of fiber and is also a fantastic way to use up that overly ripe banana.

YIELD: 6 WAFFLES | **ACTIVE TIME:** 15 MINUTES | **COOK TIME:** 10 MINUTES | **TOTAL TIME:** 25 MINUTES

Preheat a waffle iron.

In a large bowl, mix the flours, oats, and baking powder.

In a medium-size bowl, mix together the egg substitute, nondairy milk, nondairy butter, and maple syrup.

Add the banana and mix with an electric mixer on medium speed until smooth. An immersion blender will also work well.

Add the wet mixture to the dry ingredients and mix well.

Pour about ½ cup of batter into the center of the heated waffle iron and cook until done.

Serve with maple syrup and sliced bananas, if desired.

1 cup all-purpose flour

1 cup oat bran flour

¼ cup quick-cooking oats

1 teaspoon baking powder

Vegan substitute for 2 eggs, prepared

1¼ cups nondairy milk

2 tablespoons nondairy butter, melted

2 tablespoons pure maple syrup

1 ripe banana, mashed

Storing in the refrigerator:

Will keep covered in the refrigerator for up to 3 days. You can crisp them up in a toaster.

Freezing:

Freeze in either resealable plastic bags or a hard-sided freezer container for up to 3 months. Defrost in the refrigerator and heat in a toaster.

Maple Oatmeal Pancakes

Pancakes bring up memories of weekends. Maybe because they aren't the "grab and go" type of breakfast but belong to the "eat and relax over the paper" kind of morning. You don't need any syrup with these pancakes, but I understand. You decide.

YIELD: 12 TO 14 PANCAKES | **ACTIVE TIME:** 20 MINUTES | **COOK TIME:** 15 MINUTES | **TOTAL TIME:** 35 MINUTES

In a large bowl, combine the flour, oats, baking powder, and salt. Mix well.

Add the nondairy milk, maple syrup, 2 tablespoons of the coconut oil, and the egg substitute. Mix well.

Heat a little bit of the remaining oil in a 10-inch skillet. When hot, pour ¼ cup of the batter into the center of the pan and help spread it out to about a 5-inch round. Cook until small bubbles pop up all over the top of the pancake. Flip over and cook on the other side. Continue until the batter is used up.

Serve hot with more maple syrup.

1 cup whole wheat flour

1 cup rolled oats

2 teaspoons baking powder

1 teaspoon salt

1½ cups nondairy milk

¼ cup pure maple syrup

4 tablespoons coconut oil, divided

Vegan substitute for 2 eggs, prepared

Storing in the refrigerator:

Will keep tightly covered in the refrigerator for up to 4 days.

Freezing:

Freeze in either resealable plastic bags or a hard-sided freezer container for up to 3 months. Defrost in the refrigerator.

Reheating:

A nice way to reheat the pancakes is to place them in a lightly oiled and heated skillet for about 2 minutes on each side. They come out as if you just cooked them.

Banana Chocolate Chip Pancakes

These are nice tasty and fluffy pancakes with remarkable ingredients. Banana, oats, and peanut butter to start with, so why not continue on to decadence. Chocolate!

YIELD: 12 PANCAKES | **ACTIVE TIME:** 20 MINUTES | **COOK TIME:** 15 MINUTES | **TOTAL TIME:** 35 MINUTES

In a large bowl, combine the bananas, egg substitute, peanut butter, nondairy milk, baking powder, vanilla, and salt. Mix well.

Add the oats and flour and mix well. Fold in the chocolate chips.

Heat a little bit of the coconut oil in a skillet. When hot, pour ¼ cup of the batter into the center of the pan and help spread it out to about a 4-inch round. Cook until small bubbles pop up all over the top of the pancake. Flip over and cook on the other side.

Serve hot with more chocolate chips and maple syrup, if desired.

2 ripe bananas, mashed

Vegan substitute for 2 eggs, prepared

2 tablespoons peanut butter

½ cup nondairy milk

2 teaspoons baking powder

2 teaspoons vanilla extract

¼ teaspoon sea salt

1 cup rolled oats

½ cup whole wheat flour

½ cup vegan chocolate chips

2 tablespoons coconut oil

Storing in the refrigerator:

Will keep tightly covered in the refrigerator for up to 4 days.

Freezing:

Freeze in either resealable plastic bags or a hard-sided freezer container for up to 3 months. Defrost in the refrigerator.

Reheating:

A nice way to heat the pancakes is to place them in a lightly oiled and heated skillet for about 2 minutes on each side. They come out as if you just cooked them.

Extra-Special Protein Bars

Here is a great bar that is not only a very good starter for the day, but travels well as a snack, too. Lots of crunch and satisfaction all in one bar.

YIELD: 18 BARS | **ACTIVE TIME:** 20 MINUTES | **REFRIGERATOR TIME:** 4 HOURS | **TOTAL TIME:** 4 HOURS 20 MINUTES

Pour the coconut cream into a large bowl and stir well. Add the protein powder and mix until very smooth. Add the peanut butter and mix that in as well. Add the oats, chocolate chips, and cashews. Mix in very well.

Lay a piece of waxed paper across the whole width of a 9 x 13-inch pan with the edges hanging over on the far sides. These will be the "handles" to help you remove the protein bars. Pour the mixture into the pan on top of the waxed paper. Press down firmly and evenly with your fingers and palm of your hand. Refrigerate for at least 4 hours or overnight. Remove from the refrigerator and lift out, using the waxed paper. It will lift out in one block. Set on a cutting board and cut into 18 bars.

1 (13.5-ounce) can full-fat coconut cream (17% to 22% fat)

1 cup vanilla protein powder (see note)

1⅓ cups smooth peanut butter

5½ cups quick-cooking oats

1 cup vegan mini chocolate chips

1 cup cashews, chopped

NOTE:

You can use any of your favorite protein powders. I just happen to favor vanilla. The taste of the protein powder comes through strongly, so make sure it is one that you are familiar with.

Storing in the refrigerator:

Will keep covered in the refrigerator for up to 1 week.

Freezing:

Freeze in either resealable plastic bags or a hard-sided freezer container for up to 6 months.

CHAPTER THREE

To Warm You from the Inside Out

Split Pea Soup

It is true. This is the best split pea soup you will ever have. I know it is wonderful at the restaurants and the cans are even pretty good but . . . humility aside, this one is the best.

YIELD: 4 TO 6 SERVINGS | **ACTIVE TIME:** 30 MINUTES | **COOK TIME:** 1½ HOURS | **TOTAL TIME:** 2 HOURS

In a large soup pot over medium heat, heat the coconut oil and sauté the onion for about 10 minutes.

Add the split peas, vegetable stock, wine, if using, carrots, bay leaf, and pepper.

Cover and bring to a boil. Add the marjoram and parsley. Lower the heat to a medium-low simmer and cook for about 1½ hours, stirring every once in a while to keep from sticking. You can add more stock if you think it is too thick.

When the split peas are done, let the soup cool a little bit. Remove the bay leaf.

Put the soup in a blender, in two batches. Blend until the soup is smooth (or almost smooth, depending on your taste). Serve hot.

2 tablespoons coconut oil

1 small yellow onion, diced (½ to ¾ cup)

16 ounces dried green split peas

6 cups vegan vegetable stock, plus more if needed

¼ cup dry white wine (you may use water)

2 carrots, sliced (about 1 cup)

1 bay leaf

¼ teaspoon freshly ground black pepper

¼ teaspoon dried marjoram

½ teaspoon dried parsley

Storing in the refrigerator:

Will keep covered in the refrigerator for up to 4 days.

Freezing:

Let cool to room temperature. Freeze in hard-sided freezer containers for up to 3 months. To prepare after freezing, defrost in the refrigerator overnight because it is a pretty solid mass and will take longer to thaw.

Reheating:

Place in a saucepan and heat through. You can add more stock if you think it is too thick.

to warm you from the inside out

Onion Soup Spectacular

This onion soup is rich and flavorful and I could eat it every day. It is amazing how much flavor comes from this pot of soup with the little bit of cooking time that it requires.

YIELD: 4 TO 6 SERVINGS | **ACTIVE TIME:** 10 MINUTES | **COOK TIME:** 1 HOUR 10 MINUTES |
TOTAL TIME: 1 HOUR 20 MINUTES

Thinly slice the onions; you will have 5 to 6 cups.

In a large soup pot, over medium-low heat, melt the nondairy butter. Add the onions and cook, stirring often, until limp and soft, about 20 minutes. This makes the onions nice and sweet.

Turn up the heat to medium-high and cook the onions until golden brown, about 10 minutes. Do not burn.

Lower the heat to medium. Add the flour and cook for 2 minutes.

Add the vegetable stock, water, salt, wine, mustard, and bay leaf. Bring to a boil, stirring frequently. Adjust the heat to a high simmer and cook (with the lid off) for 30 more minutes.

Taste and season with more salt and pepper, if needed.

At this point you may refrigerate or freeze the soup; otherwise, ladle the soup into individual broiler-proof bowls. Bean bowls with handles are great.

Lightly lay a slice of French bread on the top of the soup. Do not push the bread down into the soup. (Alternatively, you can cut up more than one slice of bread and fit it into the bowl to cover the soup.)

Lay the sliced mozzarella cheese over the bread completely, to keep the bread from burning.

Put the bowl or bowls on a cookie sheet (two at a time for safety).

Turn on the broiler and slide your cookie sheet under the oven broiler, on the top shelf. Watch carefully—do not walk away.

Take out the pan when the cheese has lightly turned to a dark golden shade here and there.

3 large yellow onions (3 pounds)

3 tablespoons nondairy butter

4 cups vegan vegetable stock

1 cup water

2 tablespoons all-purpose flour

¼ teaspoon freshly ground black pepper

½ teaspoon sea salt

2 tablespoons dry white wine

1 teaspoon Dijon mustard

1 bay leaf

Vegan French bread, for garnish

Nondairy mozzarella cheese, sliced, for garnish

Storing in the refrigerator:

Will keep covered in the refrigerator for up to 4 days.

Freezing:

Let cool to room temperature. Freeze without the bread and cheese on top—just the basic soup. Freeze in hard-sided freezer containers for up to 3 months. To prepare after freezing, defrost in the refrigerator overnight because it is a pretty solid mass and will take longer to thaw.

Reheating:

Follow the directions above for heating through and adding the bread and cheese.

Poblano Chiles Pinto Bean Soup

Pinto bean soup begs for a big spoon. The thickness of the soup makes it very hearty, and roasting the poblano chiles adds the final touch to this deeply smoky-flavored soup.

YIELD: 4 TO 6 SERVINGS | **ACTIVE TIME:** 30 MINUTES | **COOK TIME:** 1 HOUR | **TOTAL TIME:** 1½ HOURS

Pick through the beans to make sure there are no pebbles. Rinse. Soak overnight, covered by at least 2 inches of water. The beans will swell. Drain the beans.

Pour the beans into a large soup pot. Add the vegetable stock and bring to a boil. Turn down the heat and simmer over medium heat.

Roast the poblano chiles. Place the chiles on the top rack under the broiler. Place a baking sheet on the rack below to catch the drippings. Turn on the broiler and roast the chiles, turning often with tongs, until all sides are black. Remove from the broiler and let cool until you can handle them. Rub the chiles with a damp cloth to remove the blackened skins. Seed and core because the seeds will make the soup too hot. Chop the chiles into small pieces.

In a 10-inch skillet, heat the coconut oil over medium-high heat and then add the onion. Sauté for about 10 minutes. Add the garlic and chiles and cook for a couple more minutes. Add this mixture to the pot of beans.

Add the remaining ingredients to the soup pot. Cover and cook over medium heat for about 1½ hours, stirring occasionally.

When the cooking time is done, remove about a cup of the beans. Mash them in a bowl and then return them to the bean pot. Taste for seasoning and add more salt, if needed.

16 ounces dried pinto beans

32 ounces vegan vegetable stock

16 ounces water

2 poblano chiles

1 tablespoon coconut oil

1 small white onion, chopped

3 cloves garlic, finely chopped

1 teaspoon ground cumin

½ teaspoon chili powder

¼ teaspoon paprika

1 teaspoon sea salt

¼ teaspoon freshly ground black pepper

Storing in the refrigerator:

Will keep covered in the refrigerator for 2 to 3 days.

Freezing:

Let cool to room temperature. Freeze in hard-sided freezer containers for up to 3 months. To prepare after freezing, defrost in the refrigerator overnight because it is a pretty solid mass and will take longer to thaw.

Reheating:

Place in a saucepan and heat through.

Rich Tomato Soup

There are many twists to this wonderful soup. Read on to see what I mean and you will think this soup came from one of the finest restaurants.

YIELD: 4 TO 6 SERVINGS | **ACTIVE TIME:** 30 MINUTES | **COOK TIME:** 1 HOUR | **TOTAL TIME:** 1½ HOURS

Place the coconut oil in a large soup pot and heat over medium-high heat. When the oil is hot, add the onion and sauté until translucent, about 10 minutes. Remove from the heat.

Place the soaked cashews and vegetable stock in a blender. Blend at medium-high speed until smooth. Add the sautéed onion, canned tomatoes, sun-dried tomatoes, and tomato paste. Blend again until smooth.

Pour the tomato mixture back into the soup pot and add the spices, salt, and pepper. Simmer over medium heat for 20 to 30 minutes. Serve hot.

1 tablespoon coconut oil

½ cup white onion, diced

½ cup cashews, soaked for at least 4 hours

2 cups vegan vegetable stock

2 (14.5-ounce) cans diced tomatoes

¼ cup oil-packed sun-dried tomatoes

4 tablespoons tomato paste

1 teaspoon dried oregano

½ teaspoon dried thyme

1 teaspoon sea salt

½ teaspoon freshly ground black pepper

Storing in the refrigerator:

Will keep covered in the refrigerator for up to 4 days.

Freezing:

Let cool to room temperature. Freeze in hard-sided freezer containers for up to 3 months. To prepare after freezing, defrost in the refrigerator overnight because it is a pretty solid mass and will take longer to thaw.

Reheating:

Place in a saucepan and heat through.

thyme

West African Peanut Soup

A rich soup that will make your eyes pop wide on your first sip. The depth of flavors is phenomenal.

YIELD: 4 SERVINGS | **ACTIVE TIME:** 20 MINUTES | **COOK TIME:** 1 HOUR | **TOTAL TIME:** 1 HOUR 20 MINUTES

Cook the brown rice. If you don't have a rice cooker, place the rice and 2 cups of water in a medium-size saucepan. Bring the rice to a boil over high heat. Cover the pot and let simmer over medium-high heat until the water is absorbed and the rice is tender, 40 to 50 minutes. Check that the rice is done and then remove from the heat.

In a large pan, heat the coconut oil over medium heat. Add the onion and sauté for about 10 minutes, until the onion is translucent. Add the vegetable stock and carrot and bring to a boil. Add the peanuts, tomato paste, peanut butter, hot sauce, salt, and pepper. Stir well.

Add the cooked rice and heat through. Serve hot in a bowl, with nondairy Parmesan sprinkled on top.

1 cup uncooked brown rice

1 tablespoon coconut oil

3 cups vegan vegetable stock

½ cup red onion, diced

1 cup carrot, chunked

½ cup peanuts

3 tablespoons tomato paste

¼ cup peanut butter

A couple of dashes of hot sauce

1 teaspoon sea salt

¼ teaspoon freshly ground black pepper

Nondairy Parmesan Cheese (page 131), for garnish

Storing in the refrigerator:

Will keep covered in the refrigerator for up to 4 days.

Freezing:

Let cool to room temperature. Freeze in hard-sided freezer containers for up to 3 months. To prepare after freezing, defrost in the refrigerator overnight because it is a pretty solid mass and will take longer to thaw.

Reheating:

Place in a saucepan and heat through.

to warm you from the inside out

Slow Cooker Vegan Sausage Black Bean Soup

This dressed-up black bean soup is a slow cooker dump-and-go recipe. Even with all of the spices, the balance is just right and a year-round comfort food. Use your slow cooker on the patio or deck when you don't want to heat up the house.

YIELD: 6 SERVINGS | **ACTIVE TIME:** 20 MINUTES | **COOK TIME:** 6 TO 8 HOURS | **TOTAL TIME:** 6 TO 8 HOURS 20 MINUTES

Do not presoak the black beans. Pick through the beans to make sure there are no pebbles. Rinse. Pour into a 5- to 6-quart slow cooker. Add the remaining ingredients and stir well.

Cook on LOW for 6 to 8 hours, checking the beans at 6 hours. You want them quite soft. Serve hot and, if desired, sprinkle with diced avocado.

16 ounces dried black beans

1 (10-ounce) package vegan sausage patties, cut into smaller pieces

1 small white onion, diced

2 carrots, chopped

1 cup of your favorite salsa

1 tablespoon chili powder

1 teaspoon ground cumin

1 teaspoon dried oregano

4 cups vegan vegetable stock

3 cups water

1 teaspoon sea salt

Diced avocado, for garnish (optional)

Storing in the refrigerator:

Will keep covered in the refrigerator for up to 4 days.

Freezing:

Let cool to room temperature. Freeze in hard-sided freezer containers for up to 3 months. To prepare after freezing, defrost in the refrigerator overnight because it is a pretty solid mass and will take longer to thaw.

Reheating:

Place in a saucepan and heat through.

Chili

to warm you from the inside out

Reheating:

Place in a saucepan and heat through. Garnish with avocado, parsley, and more tortilla strips.

Oaxacan Tortilla Soup

If you have never had one of the most popular soups in the Southwest, then you must try Oaxacan Tortilla Soup. Thin strips of fried corn tortillas are added to the flavorful broth, making it substantial and tasty.

YIELD: 6 SERVINGS | **ACTIVE TIME:** 20 MINUTES | **COOK TIME:** 50 MINUTES | **TOTAL TIME:** 1 HOUR 10 MINUTES

In a large stockpot, heat the coconut oil over medium-high heat. Add the tortilla strips in two batches and cook until lightly golden, about 1 minute. Drain on paper towels.

Lower the heat to medium, add the onion, and cook about 5 minutes. And the garlic and spices and cook for another 5 minutes. Add the chipotle in adobo sauce, vegetable stock, tomatoes, bay leaf, and salt. Bring to a boil, then lower the heat to simmer. Cook for 30 minutes. Remove the bay leaf.

Let cool a bit so that you can put the soup in a blender or food processor. Puree the soup in about four batches.

At this point you may refrigerate or freeze the soup; otherwise, return the pureed soup to the pot and heat through. Place some tortilla strips in each soup bowl and ladle on some soup. Garnish with diced avocado, parsley, and more tortilla strips.

4 tablespoons coconut oil

6 (6-inch) corn tortillas, cut into strips about ¼ inch wide, plus more for garnish

1 small white onion, coarsely chopped

3 cloves garlic, peeled

1 teaspoon ground cumin

1 teaspoon ground coriander

1 teaspoon chili powder

1 chipotle chile in adobo sauce

32 ounces vegan vegetable stock

1 (16-ounce) can fire-roasted tomatoes

1 bay leaf

1 teaspoon sea salt

Diced avocado, for garnish

Fresh parsley, for garnish

Storing in the refrigerator:

Will keep covered in the refrigerator for up to 4 days.

Freezing:

Let cool to room temperature. Freeze in hard-sided freezer containers for up to 3 months. To prepare after freezing, defrost in the refrigerator overnight because it is a pretty solid mass and will take longer to thaw.

Skillet Bean and Barley Soup

How fun is this? A soup made in a skillet. The ingredients are built on top of each other and the flavors mingle and blend as the soup grows.

YIELD: 4 SERVINGS | **ACTIVE TIME:** 15 MINUTES | **COOK TIME:** 40 MINUTES | **TOTAL TIME:** 55 MINUTES

In a large skillet, heat the olive oil over medium-high heat. When the oil is hot, add the onion and carrots and sauté until the onion is translucent, about 10 minutes.

Stir in the vegetable stock, tomatoes, and barley, and cook for 20 minutes. Add the beans, thyme, salt, and pepper and cook for 10 more minutes. Serve hot.

1 tablespoon olive oil

½ cup white onion, diced

1 carrot, diced

1½ cups vegan vegetable stock

1 (14.5-ounce) can diced tomatoes

¼ cup pearl barley

1 (15-ounce) can cannellini beans (white kidney beans), drained and rinsed

½ teaspoon dried thyme

1 teaspoon sea salt

¼ teaspoon freshly ground black pepper

Storing in the refrigerator:

Will keep covered in the refrigerator for up to 4 days.

Freezing:

Let cool to room temperature. Freeze in hard-sided freezer containers for up to 3 months. To prepare after freezing, defrost in the refrigerator overnight because it is a pretty solid mass and will take longer to thaw.

Reheating:

Place in a saucepan and heat through.

Creamy Mushroom Tomato Soup

Rich tomato soup is embellished with coconut cream and mushrooms. It is the perfect soup to go along with a loaf of crusty bread. You can dunk or not.

YIELD: 6 SERVINGS | **ACTIVE TIME:** 20 MINUTES | **COOK TIME:** 40 MINUTES | **TOTAL TIME:** 1 HOUR

Preheat the oven to 450°F. Lightly grease a baking sheet with coconut oil.

Cut the tomatoes in half lengthwise and cut out the very tips of the cores. Place, cut side down, on the prepared baking sheet. Brush the tomatoes with a little bit of oil and sprinkle their backs with the garlic powder, salt, basil, oregano, and pepper. Bake for 20 minutes. Let cool.

While the tomatoes are roasting, heat a tablespoon of the coconut oil in a large skillet over medium heat. When hot, add the onion and mushrooms and sauté for 10 to 15 minutes.

Scrape the tomatoes from the baking sheet into a blender. Blend at medium speed until smooth.

To the skillet holding the mushroom mixture, add the vegetable stock, tomato paste, and blended tomatoes. Bring to a boil and then remove from the heat. Add the nondairy milk and make sure the soup is heated through. Serve hot and sprinkle with chives.

2 pounds plum tomatoes

2 tablespoons coconut oil, plus more for baking sheet

¼ teaspoon garlic powder

½ teaspoon salt

½ teaspoon dried basil

½ teaspoon dried oregano

½ teaspoon freshly ground black pepper

10 ounces button mushrooms, sliced

½ cup white onion, diced

2 cups vegan vegetable stock

¼ cup tomato paste

1 cup nondairy milk

Chopped chives, for garnish

Storing in the refrigerator:

Will keep covered in the refrigerator for 2 to 3 days.

Freezing:

Let cool to room temperature. Freeze in hard-sided freezer containers for up to 3 months. To prepare after freezing, defrost in the refrigerator overnight because it is a pretty solid mass and will take longer to thaw.

Reheating:

Place in a saucepan and heat through.

to warm you from the inside out

Italian Cannellini Soup

A few of the beans are mashed and then added back into the soup to make a thick, creamy texture. This is a great soup for a cold day.

YIELD: 10 SERVINGS | **ACTIVE TIME:** 15 MINUTES | **COOK TIME:** 1 HOUR 45 MINUTES | **TOTAL TIME:** 2 HOURS

Pick through the beans to make sure there are no pebbles. Rinse. Soak overnight, covered by at least 2 inches of water. They will swell.

In a soup pot, heat the coconut oil over medium-high heat. When the oil is hot, add the onion and sauté for about 10 minutes. Add the garlic and cook for another minute.

Drain the beans and pour into the soup pot. Add the remaining ingredients. Bring to a boil, then cover and lower heat. Cook at a medium simmer for 1½ hours, stirring occasionally. Check the beans after 1 hour. Discard the bay leaf.

Serve with a big loaf of crusty vegan Italian bread.

1 cup dried cannellini beans

1 cup dried kidney beans

1 tablespoon coconut oil

½ cup yellow onion, diced

1 clove garlic, finely chopped

1 (28-ounce) can crushed tomatoes, or about 4 fresh tomatoes, finely chopped

32 ounces vegan vegetable stock

3 carrots, diced

1 bay leaf

1 teaspoon dried oregano

1 teaspoon sea salt

¼ teaspoon freshly ground black pepper

Storing in the refrigerator:

Will keep covered in the refrigerator for 2 to 3 days.

Freezing:

Let cool to room temperature. Freeze in hard-sided freezer containers for up to 3 months. To prepare after freezing, defrost in the refrigerator overnight because it is a pretty solid mass and will take longer to thaw.

Reheating:

Place in a large saucepan and heat through.

Tuscan Ditalini Soup

Minestrone soup got all dressed up for this recipe. The standard is always great, but why not take it up another notch?

YIELD: 4 SERVINGS | **ACTIVE TIME:** 20 MINUTES | **COOK TIME:** 20 MINUTES | **TOTAL TIME:** 40 MINUTES

In a large pot, heat the coconut oil over medium-high heat. Add the onion and sauté for about 10 minutes, or until translucent in color. Add the garlic and cook for just a minute or two. Add the vegetable stock, tomatoes, red bell pepper, wine, oregano, and basil.

Mash half of the beans in a small bowl. Bring the soup to a boil and add the pasta and all the beans.

Lower the heat to medium-high and cook the soup for 6 to 8 minutes. You are looking for al dente pasta.

Add the salt and black pepper, stir, and then taste for seasoning.

1 tablespoon coconut oil

1 cup white onion, diced

2 cloves garlic, minced

32 ounces vegan vegetable stock

1 (15-ounce) can diced tomatoes, or 3 fresh tomatoes, diced

¼ cup roasted red bell pepper, chopped small

¼ cup dry red wine, such as burgundy

1 teaspoon dried oregano

1 teaspoon dried basil

1 (15-ounce) can cannellini beans, drained and rinsed

8 ounces ditalini pasta

1 teaspoon sea salt

¼ teaspoon freshly ground black pepper

Storing in the refrigerator:

Will keep covered in the refrigerator for up to 4 days.

Freezing:

Let cool to room temperature. Freeze in hard-sided freezer containers for up to 3 months. To prepare after freezing, defrost in the refrigerator overnight because it is a pretty solid mass and will take longer to thaw.

Reheating:

Place in a saucepan and heat through.

to warm you from the inside out

Slow Cooker Vegetable Stew

Ease of preparation and an abundance of vegetables are the mainstay to this hearty main dish stew.

YIELD: 6 SERVINGS | **ACTIVE TIME:** 20 MINUTES | **COOK TIME:** 6 TO 8 HOURS | **TOTAL TIME:** 6 TO 8 HOURS 20 MINUTES

Pick through the beans to make sure there are no pebbles. Rinse. Soak the beans overnight, covered by at least 2 inches of water. The beans will swell.

In the morning, drain the beans and pour into a 5- to 7-quart slow cooker.

Add all the remaining ingredients and cook on LOW for 6 to 8 hours. Check at 6 hours; it may be done to your liking. The soup will keep in the slow cooker for up to 1½ hours.

16 ounces dried great northern beans

1 small white onion, diced

64 ounces vegan vegetable stock

1 russet potato, chopped

1 ear of corn, kernels cut off the cob

2 large carrots, chopped

1 (14.5-ounce) can diced tomatoes

½ teaspoon dried basil

½ teaspoon dried oregano

⅛ teaspoon ground allspice

2 bay leaves

1 teaspoon sea salt

¼ teaspoon freshly ground black pepper

Storing in the refrigerator:

Will keep covered in the refrigerator for up to 4 days.

Freezing:

Let cool to room temperature. Freeze in hard-sided freezer containers for up to 3 months. To prepare after freezing, defrost in the refrigerator overnight because it is a pretty solid mass and will take longer to thaw.

Reheating:

Place in a saucepan and heat through.

White Bean Chili

White bean chili is a very nice change from the heavier red bean chili. It is completely different in flavor with mild green chiles and select spices.

YIELD: 6 SERVINGS | **ACTIVE TIME:** 15 MINUTES | **COOK TIME:** 1 HOUR 20 MINUTES | **TOTAL TIME:** 1 HOUR 35 MINUTES

Pick through the beans to make sure there are no pebbles. Rinse. Soak overnight, covered by at least 2 inches of water. The beans will swell. Drain the beans.

Pour the beans into a large soup pot. Add the vegetable stock and bring to a boil. Lower the heat and simmer over medium heat.

In a saucepan, heat the coconut oil over medium-high heat. When the oil is hot, add the onion. Sauté for about 10 minutes. Add the garlic and chiles and cook for a couple more minutes. Add the vegetable mixture to the beans.

Add the remaining ingredients to the soup pot. Cover and cook over medium heat for about 1½ hours, stirring occasionally.

This soup goes really well with corn bread.

16 ounces dried navy beans

6 cups vegan vegetable stock

1 tablespoon coconut oil

1 small yellow onion, diced

3 to 4 cloves garlic, finely chopped

1 (4-ounce) can mild green chiles

1 tablespoon nutritional yeast

2 teaspoons ground cumin

1½ teaspoons dried oregano

½ teaspoon cayenne pepper

¼ teaspoon ground cloves

1 teaspoon sea salt

Pinch of freshly ground black pepper

Storing in the refrigerator:

Will keep covered in the refrigerator for 2 to 3 days.

Freezing:

Let cool to room temperature. Freeze in hard-sided freezer containers for up to 3 months. To prepare after freezing, defrost in the refrigerator overnight because it is a pretty solid mass and will take longer to thaw.

Reheating:

Place in a saucepan and heat through.

to warm you from the inside out

Win the Chili Contest Chili

Who doesn't want to have the best chili recipe? This is quick because it takes advantage of canned goods; after making this recipe, you will have bragging rights.

YIELD: 6 SERVINGS | **ACTIVE TIME:** 15 MINUTES | **COOK TIME:** 45 MINUTES | **TOTAL TIME:** 1 HOUR

In a large pot, heat the coconut oil over medium-high heat. When the oil is hot, add the onion, red bell pepper, and green bell pepper and sauté for 10 to 15 minutes, until the onion is translucent and the peppers are limp. Add the garlic and cook for 1 more minute.

Add all the remaining ingredients. Stir well and bring to a boil. Lower the heat, cover, and simmer for 30 minutes.

2 tablespoons coconut oil

1 white onion, diced

1 red bell pepper, diced

1 green bell pepper, diced

3 cloves garlic, finely chopped

1 (10-ounce) package vegan sausage patties, chopped into smaller pieces

2 (28-ounce) cans diced tomatoes

1 (15-ounce) can tomato sauce

1 (15-ounce) can kidney beans, drained and rinsed

1 (15-ounce) can pinto beans, drained and rinsed

2 tablespoons chili powder

1 teaspoon ground cumin

1 teaspoon dried oregano

2 tablespoons coconut sugar

1 teaspoon sea salt

Storing in the refrigerator:

Will keep covered in the refrigerator for 2 to 3 days.

Freezing:

Let cool to room temperature. Freeze in hard-sided freezer containers for up to 3 months. To prepare after freezing, defrost in the refrigerator overnight because it is a pretty solid mass and will take longer to thaw.

Reheating:

Place in a saucepan and heat through.

Oregano

CHAPTER FOUR

Side Dishes to Complement

Sweet Potato Chili Logs

Sweet potatoes are made special for this spicy side dish. After some mixing and rolling, they end up being tasty and cute. All at the same time.

YIELD: 4 SERVINGS | **ACTIVE TIME:** 30 MINUTES | **COOK TIME:** 30 MINUTES | **TOTAL TIME:** 1 HOUR

Peel and chop the sweet potatoes.

Place a large pan of covered water on the stovetop and bring to a boil. When boiling, put in the sweet potatoes. Bring back to a boil and cook for about 3 minutes. Remove from the heat and drain. Put the sweet potatoes in a large bowl and mash with a potato masher.

Add the onion, flour, and seasonings. Mix well.

Form into small balls. You will get 48 to 60 balls.

Heat the coconut oil in a large, deep skillet. You want it deep enough that you only have to turn the logs once. When the oil is hot enough, slightly roll a sweet potato ball into a cigar shape. Place in the hot oil. You can do about 10 logs at a time; do not crowd.

When you see the bottom of the logs starting to turn golden, turn over each log once so that they cook on the other side. They take 1 to 2 minutes on each side. Transfer to paper towels to drain. Wash your hands and proceed with the next batch.

Serve alone or with any condiment that you like.

2 large sweet potatoes (about 2 pounds)

¼ cup white onion, finely diced

2 tablespoons all-purpose flour

1 teaspoon garlic powder

1 tablespoon chili powder

1 teaspoon sea salt

¼ teaspoon freshly ground black pepper

1 cup coconut oil, for frying

Storing in the refrigerator:

Will keep covered in the refrigerator for 2 to 3 days.

Freezing:

Let cool to room temperature. Freeze in hard-sided freezer containers for up to 3 months. To prepare after freezing, defrost in the refrigerator. That will take a couple of hours.

Reheating:

Place on a baking sheet and bake at 350°F for 8 to 10 minutes.

Green Bean Casserole

We all need a green bean casserole recipe in our recipe box. This casserole offers fresh mushrooms along with the portobello soup. It's topped with homemade onion rings, too.

YIELD: 4 SERVINGS | **ACTIVE TIME:** 40 MINUTES | **COOK TIME:** 1 HOUR | **TOTAL TIME:** 1 HOUR 40 MINUTES

Lightly grease a 1½-quart baking dish with the coconut oil.

In a large skillet, melt the nondairy butter over medium-high heat. Sauté the onion and mushrooms for about 10 minutes.

Pour the vegetable stock into a large saucepan and add the green beans. Bring to a boil. Lower the heat to medium-high and cook for 10 minutes. Drain.

Add the green beans to the mushroom mixture. Add the mushroom soup, bread crumbs, salt, and pepper and stir well.

Pour into the prepared baking dish and even out the top.

Bake for 20 minutes. Sprinkle with the Parmesan and top with onion rings.

1 tablespoon coconut oil, for baking dish

1 tablespoon nondairy butter

½ cup white onion, diced

8 ounces cremini mushrooms, sliced

3 cups vegan vegetable stock

2 cups fresh green beans, snapped

1 cup vegan portobello mushroom soup

½ cup dried vegan bread crumbs

1 teaspoon salt

¼ teaspoon freshly ground black pepper

½ cup Nondairy Parmesan Cheese (recipe follows)

Homemade Onion Rings (recipe follows)

Nondairy Parmesan Cheese

1 cup raw cashews

¼ cup nutritional yeast

½ teaspoon sea salt

¼ teaspoon garlic powder

Place all the ingredients into a food processor.

Pulse until a fine crumb forms. This will take literally seconds.

Use in just about any savory dish you can think of.

Will keep in the refrigerator for about 1 month, or in the freezer in a freezer container for up to 1 year.

Homemade Onion Rings

1 onion, thinly sliced into rings

1 cup nondairy milk

½ cup all-purpose flour

1 tablespoon garlic powder

2 teaspoons paprika

¼ teaspoon salt

⅛ teaspoon cayenne pepper

¼ cup coconut oil, for frying

Soak the onion rings in the nondairy milk.

Combine the flour and seasonings in a large bowl. Mix well.

Heat the coconut oil in a large skillet over medium-high heat.

Take the onion rings out of the nondairy milk and shake off the excess nondairy milk. Toss the rings in the flour mixture. Lay a few rings in the hot oil so that they do not overlap. Cook for about 4 minutes, flipping once during the cooking period. When the onion rings start to brown, transfer them to a paper towel to drain. Repeat until all the onion rings are fried, adding more oil if needed.

Storing in the refrigerator:

You may prepare this casserole ahead, omitting the Parmesan and onion rings; do not bake. It will keep in the refrigerator for 2 days.

Freezing:

You may prepare this casserole ahead, omitting the Parmesan and onion rings; do not bake. Pack the casserole in a freezer-safe casserole that can also go in the oven. It will keep 3 months in the freezer. To prepare after freezing, defrost in the refrigerator overnight.

Baking after storage:

Bake at 350°F for 30 minutes. Sprinkle the Parmesan over the top and top with onion rings.

side dishes to complement

Freezing:

You may prepare this casserole ahead, but do not bake it. Pack the casserole in a freezer-safe casserole that can also go in the oven. It will keep for 3 months in the freezer. To prepare after freezing, defrost in the refrigerator overnight.

Creamy Broccoli Bake

There are many ingredients in this casserole and many are scant measurements. All are necessary for the depth and balance of flavors. Use a big serving spoon to scoop up the saucy goodness.

YIELD: 6 SERVINGS | **ACTIVE TIME:** 40 MINUTES | **COOK TIME:** 1 HOUR | **TOTAL TIME:** 1 HOUR 40 MINUTES

Lightly grease a 2-quart casserole with coconut oil.

Cook the brown rice. If you don't have a rice cooker, place the rice and 4 cups of water in a medium-size saucepan. Bring the rice to a boil over high heat. Cover the pot and let simmer over medium-high heat until the water is absorbed and the rice is tender, 40 to 50 minutes. Check that the rice is done and then remove from the heat.

To make the sauce: In a blender, combine the nondairy milk, nutritional yeast, cornstarch, wine, garlic powder, onion powder, salt, black pepper, paprika, and mustard. Blend at medium speed until smooth.

Place the broccoli florets in a steamer basket and steam for 5 to 8 minutes. They will not be completely cooked yet. Remove from the pan to stop the cooking.

Heat the coconut oil to a large skillet over medium-high heat. Add the onion and red bell pepper and sauté for 10 minutes. Stir in the cooked rice, broccoli, oregano, cashews, and the sauce from the blender. Stir to combine the sauce with all the other ingredients.

Pour into the prepared casserole dish. At this point you may refrigerate or freeze the casserole; otherwise, preheat the oven to 350°F.

Bake for 25 minutes.

- 1 tablespoon coconut oil, plus more for casserole
- 2 cups uncooked brown rice
- 1½ cups nondairy milk
- ½ cup nutritional yeast
- 1 tablespoon cornstarch
- 1 tablespoon white wine
- ½ teaspoon garlic powder
- ½ teaspoon onion powder
- ½ teaspoon sea salt
- ¼ teaspoon freshly ground black pepper
- ¼ teaspoon sweet paprika
- ⅛ teaspoon dry mustard
- 1 head broccoli, cut into small florets
- ½ cup white onion, diced
- ½ cup red bell pepper, diced
- ½ teaspoon dried oregano
- ½ cup cashews

Storing in the refrigerator:

You may prepare this casserole ahead, but do not bake it. It will keep in the refrigerator for 2 days.

Baking after storing:

Bake in a 350°F oven for 25 minutes.

French Onion Casserole

Simple is as simple does. That is my motto for this recipe. A few ingredients, two snaps of the fingers, and you have an enjoyable and satisfying side dish.

YIELD: 4 SERVINGS | ACTIVE TIME: 5 MINUTES | COOK TIME: 1 HOUR | TOTAL TIME: 1 HOUR 5 MINUTES

Preheat the oven to 375°F.

Place all the ingredients in an 8 x 8-inch casserole and stir. Bake for 1 hour.

10 ounces vegan vegetable stock

1 (10-ounce) can vegan onion soup

½ cup (1 stick, 4 ounces) nondairy butter, melted

1 cup uncooked long-grain rice

Storing in the refrigerator:

This baked casserole will keep in the refrigerator for 3 to 4 days. Heat through in the microwave.

Freezing:

This casserole can be frozen after it is baked. Freeze in smaller containers and it will keep for 3 months in the freezer. To prepare after freezing, defrost in the refrigerator overnight.

Reheating:

Depending on the size you are heating, microwave on medium power for 2 to 4 minutes, stirring every 30 seconds.

Slow Cooker Refried Beans

Now you can make a big pot of refried beans with no additives, preservatives, or extra fats. Make enough to freeze and it will always be on hand.

YIELD: 6 SERVINGS | **ACTIVE TIME:** 20 MINUTES | **COOK TIME:** 3 HOURS | **TOTAL TIME:** 3 HOURS 20 MINUTES

Pick through the beans to make sure there are no pebbles. Rinse. Put the beans in a large pot with water to cover (about 6 cups of water). Let the pot sit all day or overnight and the beans will plump up. Drain the beans and pour them into a 4½-quart slow cooker. Cover with fresh water by 1 to 2 inches. Cook on HIGH for 3 hours.

While the beans are cooking, prepare the vegetables: In a large skillet, heat the olive oil over medium heat. Add the onion and sauté until translucent. Add the garlic and chile pepper. Cook for 2 more minutes. Add all the seasonings to the pan. Cook for another minute, stirring occasionally. Set aside.

When the beans are done, mash in the slow cooker with a potato masher. Add the onion mixture and mix well. If it is too dry, you can add some more water. Turn the slow cooker back on to the LOW setting. Cook for 1 hour.

That's it! The best refried beans and so much healthier than the canned kind.

NOTE:

If you need to add more liquid at the last hour of the final cooking process, you can add some tomato juice or diced tomatoes. Even a little salsa can be added if your family likes the extra spices.

16 ounces dried pinto beans

2 tablespoons olive oil

1 small onion, finely diced

4 cloves garlic, finely diced

1 chile pepper, finely diced

1 teaspoon ground cumin

½ teaspoon dried oregano

½ teaspoon chili powder

1 teaspoon salt

Storing in the refrigerator:

The refried beans will keep in the refrigerator for 4 days.

Freezing:

Freeze in hard-sided freezer containers for up to 6 months. To prepare after freezing, defrost in the refrigerator overnight because it is a pretty solid mass and will take longer to thaw.

Reheating:

Heat, covered, in a microwave or in a saucepan. Add a little more liquid if it seems too dry.

Baby Corn Stir-Fry

Baby corn really is immature corn, picked just as the kernels start to form off the top of six-foot stalks. Luckily for us, they come in little jars and cans at the grocery store.

YIELD: 6 SERVINGS | **ACTIVE TIME:** 15 MINUTES | **COOK TIME:** 20 MINUTES | **TOTAL TIME:** 35 MINUTES

Heat the coconut oil in a skillet over medium-high heat. When the oil is hot, add the bell peppers, mushrooms, and carrot and sauté for about 10 minutes. Add the baby corn and cook for another 5 minutes. Stir in the chili powder, hoisin sauce, and salt. Heat through and serve.

2 tablespoons coconut oil

1 red bell pepper, cut into thin strips

1 green bell pepper, cut into thin strips

12 ounces cremini mushrooms, sliced

1 carrot, cut into ¼-inch strips

1 (10-ounce) can baby corn, drained and rinsed

1 teaspoon chili powder

2 tablespoons hoisin sauce

½ teaspoon salt

Storing in the refrigerator:
Will keep covered in the refrigerator for 2 to 3 days.

Freezing:
Let cool to room temperature. Freeze in hard-sided freezer containers for up to 3 months. To prepare after freezing, defrost in the refrigerator overnight.

Reheating:
Place in a skillet and heat through.

Mashed Potato Casserole

You can't go wrong with mashed potatoes. Dairy-free cream cheese with chives and garlic adds a lot of flavor. When you have more time, you can make it ahead as an easy side dish for dinner.

YIELD: 6 SERVINGS | **ACTIVE TIME:** 20 MINUTES | **COOK TIME:** 30 MINUTES | **TOTAL TIME:** 50 MINUTES

With the coconut oil, lightly grease a large casserole (I used an 8 x 12-inch) or two smaller ones that are about 8 x 8 inches.

Peel and cut the potatoes into quarters. Put in a large saucepan and cover with water. Bring to a boil, then lower the heat to medium-high but keep it at a low boil. Cook for about 15 minutes, until you can easily pierce the potatoes with a fork. Drain the potatoes and put them back into the pan. Mash with a potato masher.

Add the remaining ingredients, except 1 tablespoon of the nondairy butter and the paprika, and mix well.

Spread the potato mixture in the prepared casserole or casseroles. At this point you may refrigerate or freeze the casserole; otherwise, preheat the oven to 350°F.

Bake for 30 minutes. Meanwhile, melt the remaining tablespoon of nondairy butter.

Drizzle the melted nondairy butter over the top and sprinkle with the paprika for looks.

1 tablespoon coconut oil

3 to 4 pounds Yukon gold potatoes

4 ounces nondairy cream cheese with chives and garlic

½ cup nondairy milk

3 tablespoons nondairy butter, divided

1 teaspoon salt

¼ teaspoon freshly ground black pepper

½ teaspoon sweet paprika

Storing in the refrigerator:

Will keep covered in the refrigerator for 2 to 3 days. You can keep in the refrigerator before or after baking.

Freezing:

Freeze before baking. Make sure the potatoes are in a freezer-to-oven-safe casserole. Freeze for up to 3 months. To prepare after freezing, defrost in the refrigerator overnight.

Baking after storing:

Bake at 350°F for 35 minutes. Drizzle the melted nondairy butter over the top and sprinkle with the paprika for looks.

Paprika

Cauliflower Tots

One head of cauliflower makes a lot of tots and they are just delicious. It takes some time to prepare them because of the rolling, but they are so worth it.

YIELD: 55 TO 65 TOTS | **ACTIVE TIME:** 40 MINUTES | **COOK TIME:** 20 MINUTES | **TOTAL TIME:** 1 HOUR

Put the cauliflower in a food processor and process until the cauliflower is in small pieces that almost look like rice. Lay a double layer of paper towels on the counter and spread the cauliflower on top. Press down evenly over the cauliflower with more paper towels to remove as much excess liquid as possible.

Mix all the ingredients, except the oil, in a large bowl. Form into small oval balls; you will get 55 to 65 tots.

Heat the coconut oil in a large skillet over medium-high heat. When the oil is hot, start adding the cauliflower tots and fry on all sides. Do not crowd. Transfer to paper towels to drain. Proceed until all the tots are fried.

Serve as a side dish or as an appetizer with a dipping sauce. They are good at room temperature, too.

1 head cauliflower, cleaned and roughly chopped

½ cup white onion, diced

¼ cup nutritional yeast

1 (15-ounce) can chickpeas, drained, rinsed, and mashed

1½ cups dried vegan bread crumbs

1 teaspoon sea salt

¼ teaspoon freshly ground black pepper

¼ cup coconut oil

Storing in the refrigerator:

Will keep covered in the refrigerator for 3 to 4 days.

Freezing:

Freeze in hard-sided freezer containers for up to 3 months to help hold their shape. To prepare after freezing, defrost in the refrigerator overnight.

Reheating:

Heat on a baking sheet in a 350°F oven for 10 minutes.

Lentil Salad

You will be amazed at what I am going to tell you. First, when you make this recipe, you have a fresh and tasty salad. If there are leftovers, the salad can be frozen. After it is defrosted, it is not salad but becomes the most wonderful base for a soup. Amazing!

YIELD: 4 SERVINGS | **ACTIVE TIME:** 40 MINUTES | **COOK TIME:** 20 MINUTES | **TOTAL TIME:** 1 HOUR

Pick through the lentils to make sure there are no pebbles. Rinse. In a large saucepan, cover the lentils with boiling water and let soak for 1½ hours. Drain and add the vegetable stock, onion, and shallot. Bring to a boil and simmer for 10 minutes, or until the lentils are done but still firm. Do not overcook. Drain.

Stir in the hot sauce, salt, and pepper. Let cool completely. Stir in the water chestnuts.

16 ounces dried brown lentils

2 cups vegan vegetable stock

1 red onion, diced

1 shallot, finely diced

¼ teaspoon hot sauce

1 teaspoon sea salt

¼ teaspoon freshly ground black pepper

1 (8-ounce) can water chestnuts, sliced

Storing in the refrigerator:

Will keep covered in the refrigerator for 3 to 4 days.

Freezing:

Freeze in freezer bag or hard-sided freezer containers for up to 4 months. To prepare after freezing, add to any homemade soup of your choice.

Balsamic Roasted Broccoli

A very quick and satisfying vegetable side dish. Rich balsamic flavors are enhanced with freshly roasted garlic.

YIELD: 6 TO 8 SERVINGS | **ACTIVE TIME:** 15 MINUTES | **COOK TIME:** 15 MINUTES | **TOTAL TIME:** 30 MINUTES

Have ready a baking pan that measures about 10 x 13 inches.

Combine the coconut oil, garlic, salt, and pepper in a large bowl. Put the broccoli in the bowl and lightly toss to evenly coat the broccoli as best you can.

Spread out the broccoli on the baking sheet. At this point you may refrigerate or freeze the broccoli; otherwise, preheat the oven to 425°F.

Bake for 7 minutes and then flip the spears with a spatula. Bake for another 8 to 10 minutes, or until you can pierce a broccoli spear easily with a fork. Remove from the oven. Drizzle the balsamic vinegar over the broccoli and toss. Serve hot.

¼ cup coconut oil

4 cloves garlic, finely diced

½ teaspoon sea salt

¼ teaspoon freshly ground black pepper

2 bunches broccoli woody ends and leaves trimmed, cut into florets with the spears attached (see "Freezing" below, if you wish to freeze the broccoli before serving)

2 tablespoons balsamic vinegar

NOTE:

You can also do this with a half-broccoli and half-cauliflower mixture.

Storing in the refrigerator:

Will keep covered in the refrigerator for 3 to 4 days before roasting.

Freezing:

You will need to freeze the broccoli before combining with the other ingredients for roasting. After cutting the broccoli as described, place into boiling water and boil for 3 to 5 minutes. Remove the vegetables from the boiling water and plunge into ice cold water to stop the cooking process. Drain the broccoli and pack into freezer bags for up to 4 months.

Reheating:

When you want to prepare the recipe for Balsamic Roasted Broccoli, take the broccoli out of the freezer and defrost in the refrigerator for at least 6 hours. Continue with the recipe as if the broccoli was fresh.

Baking or reheating:

If the risotto was refrigerated or frozen before baking, bake 50 to 55 minutes at 400°F until all of the liquid is absorbed.

If the risotto was refrigerated or frozen after baking microwave on medium power for 2 minutes. Stir and microwave for another 2 minutes. If it seems too dry, you can add a little vegetable stock.

Roasted Tomato and Baked Risotto

Risotto is turned into an easy casserole for this recipe. Roasted tomatoes brighten up the rice and you get to walk away while it bakes, instead of standing over the stovetop.

YIELD: 8 SERVINGS | **ACTIVE TIME:** 20 MINUTES | **COOK TIME:** 1 HOUR | **TOTAL TIME:** 1 HOUR 20 MINUTES

Cut the tomatoes and scoop out the seeds. If the stem end is rough, cut it out also. Now chop the tomatoes. Drizzle the coconut oil over the tomatoes and lightly toss. Place on an aluminum foil–covered baking sheet. Sprinkle with salt and pepper. Roast for 10 to 15 minutes, or until some of the edges are browned. Remove from the oven and set aside.

Turn down the oven to temperature to 375°F.

In a large, lidded ovenproof skillet or pot, melt the nondairy butter over medium-high heat. Sauté the onion for about 10 minutes, or until is translucent. Add the rice, ½ teaspoon of sea salt, and ¼ teaspoon of pepper. Cook, stirring, for 3 to 5 minutes.

Stir in the roasted tomatoes and heated liquids. Stir, cover, and bring to a boil.

At this point you may refrigerate the risotto; otherwise, preheat the oven to 400°F.

Slide the covered pot into the oven without lifting the lid.

Bake for 40 to 45 minutes, until all of the liquid is absorbed. The risotto is ready to serve.

8 to 10 Roma tomatoes, depending on their size

2 tablespoons coconut oil

Sea salt

Freshly ground black pepper

1 teaspoon nondairy butter

½ cup white onion, diced

2 cups uncooked short-grain brown rice

32 ounces vegan vegetable stock, microwaved on high power to about 150°F

¼ cup water, microwaved on high power to about 150°F

Storing in the refrigerator:

Will keep covered in the refrigerator for 3 to 4 days before baking.

Freezing:

Let cool to room temperature. Freeze in freezer bags or hard-sided freezer containers for up to 3 months. To prepare after freezing, defrost in the refrigerator overnight.

Wild Rice Blend and Mushroom Casserole

The wild rice blends in the grocery stores are such a nice option. Besides being pretty, the mixes are really well balanced. Take advantage of one for this recipe and enjoy a special side dish.

YIELD: 6 TO 8 SERVINGS | **ACTIVE TIME:** 30 MINUTES | **COOK TIME:** 20 MINUTES | **TOTAL TIME:** 50 MINUTES

Cook the wild rice blend according to directions on the package. Set aside.

Melt the nondairy butter in a large skillet and add the onion. Cook over medium heat for 5 minutes.

Add the bell pepper and mushrooms and cook for 15 more minutes.

Stir in the nutritional yeast and the seasonings. Taste to see whether you would like more salt or pepper.

Turn into a quart-size casserole and cover tightly with a lid or foil. At this point you may refrigerate or freeze the casserole; otherwise, preheat the oven to 350°F.

Bake for 20 minutes.

1 cup wild rice blend

4 tablespoons nondairy butter

1 white onion, chopped

1 green bell pepper, seeded and chopped

8 ounces button mushrooms, sliced

2 teaspoons nutritional yeast

½ teaspoon dried thyme

1 teaspoon salt

¼ teaspoon freshly ground black pepper

Storing in the refrigerator:

Will keep covered in the refrigerator for up to 3 days before or after baking.

Freezing:

You can freeze this casserole before or after baking for up to 4 months. Make sure it is a freezer-safe container with a tight-fitting lid. If you are freezing before baking, freeze in casserole dishes that can slide into large freezer bags. The leftovers can be frozen in small servings for easy reheating.

Reheating:

Heat leftovers in a microwave on medium power for 2 minutes, stirring every 30 seconds. If you have not baked the casserole yet, defrost in the refrigerator overnight. Bake in the oven, covered with lid or tightly fitting foil, at 350°F for 20 minutes. Check to make sure it is hot enough. You may have to go to 25 minutes.

Tamari Green Beans Stir-Fry

Kids love soy sauce. Have you ever noticed? Tamari is also a type of soy sauce, but it is almost always gluten-free. No wheat, a richer flavor, less salty, and the kids still love it. The slivered almonds are a nice touch, too.

YIELD: 4 SERVINGS | **ACTIVE TIME:** 15 MINUTES | **COOK TIME:** 10 MINUTES | **TOTAL TIME:** 25 MINUTES

Steam the green beans in a steamer basket for 5 minutes.

In a small bowl, mix together the almonds, tamari, wine, sugar, salt, and sesame oil.

If you are freezing the mixture, this is the point where you would stop. See the directions for stir-frying after freezing.

Otherwise, continue by heating the peanut oil in a wok or large skillet over medium-high heat. Carefully add the green beans so that you do not get splattered with hot oil. Stir and turn over the beans for about 4 minutes.

Add the tamari mixture and stir to heat through for about 30 seconds. The dish is ready to serve.

1 pound fresh green beans, snapped

¼ cup almonds, chopped

1 tablespoon tamari

1 tablespoon dry white wine

1 teaspoon raw sugar

1 teaspoon sea salt

½ teaspoon sesame oil

1 tablespoon peanut oil

Storing in the refrigerator:

This side dish will keep in the refrigerator for up to 3 days but is best when served immediately.

Freezing:

Combine the green beans and the tamari mixture. Freeze in freezer bags or hard-sided freezer containers for up to 4 months.

Stir-frying after freezing:

Defrost in the refrigerator for 4 to 6 hours. Stir-fry in the hot peanut oil as directed above.

Freezing Potatoes for Hash Browns

Sometimes it is so nice to have something quick and handy to add to your dinner menu. Fresh homemade hash browns is a great option. Whether you grate your potatoes or use a spiralizer, the outcome is clean, fresh, and delicious.

YIELD: 4 SERVINGS | **ACTIVE TIME:** 30 MINUTES | **COOK TIME:** 15 MINUTES | **TOTAL TIME:** 45 MINUTES

You will need two baking sheets, for quick freezing, and paper towels.

Potatoes turn brown fast, so to have nice white hash browns, you must follow these directions.

Fill up a large bowl with ice. Cover about halfway with water. Because the water will rise when you put in the potatoes, keep the water level down a bit so that the bowl does not overflow.

Peel and grate (or spiralize) one potato at a time. You are only going to work with two potatoes for each complete process. Place the grated potato in the ice water as quickly as you can and make sure it is all covered. I use a spiralizer half the time and if you do, too, then when the potatoes are in the water, take your kitchen scissors and cut 10 to 15 times straight down through all the spiralized potato. You don't have to be careful for sizing. A few clips and you have nice pieces. When both potatoes are grated, lay out a double layer of paper towels. Take a handful of grated potato and lay it across the paper towel. Roll up tight and squeeze out the excess water. Set aside and repeat with the rest of the grated potatoes. There will be three to four handfuls to squeeze out.

Unroll the potatoes and dump onto one of the baking sheets. Spread out evenly and immediately place in the freezer. Leave these for about an hour so that they become frozen.

Continue, doing the exact same process with the next two potatoes.

4 russet potatoes

When the freezing time is over, remove the pans from the freezer. Your perfectly white hash browns are ready for bagging up. Take a spatula and loosen the potatoes from the pans. Place all of the potatoes in a freezer bag. Roll up to get out all the extra air, then seal. Place in another freezer bag and roll the same way.

This is a great method because you do not have to blanch the potatoes first. Because of this, you do need to use them faster, though. They will keep for 1 to 2 months in the freezer.

Preparing the frozen potatoes:

Heat about 3 tablespoons of coconut oil in a skillet that has a lid. When the oil is hot, carefully drop in about three handfuls of frozen hash browns. Spread out evenly in the pan, but not more than ¼ to ½ inch deep. Cover and let cook for 5 to 7 minutes. The potatoes will shrink a bit when they are cooking. You will be tempted to stir and flip, but don't. After the potatoes look golden brown on the underside, flip once with a spatula (do not stir) and cook, uncovered, until the other side browns. This will also take 5 to 7 minutes. Drain on a paper towel and salt lightly. Serve hot.

Fresh Corn with Chipotle Maple Sauce

The sweet and hot contrast for this corn and carrot side dish is a winner. Chipotles in adobo sauce is so popular and one of the reasons is the depth of flavors that is added to a recipe. There is no exception here.

YIELD: 6 TO 8 SERVINGS | **ACTIVE TIME:** 25 MINUTES | **COOK TIME:** 5 MINUTES | **TOTAL TIME:** 30 MINUTES

Place the corn in a large pot and add cold water to cover. Bring to a boil, then turn off the heat. Let the corn soak in the hot water for 10 minutes. Remove from the water and cut the kernels off the cobs.

While the water is coming to a boil, place the carrot chunks in a medium-size saucepan. Cover with cold water by about 2 inches. Cover and bring to a boil. Tilt the lid so that some air gets in and lower the heat to medium. Cook for 20 minutes, or until a fork can be inserted in a carrot chunk.

Meanwhile, in a small saucepan, combine the maple syrup, nondairy butter, chipotles, salt, and pepper. Over medium-high heat, stir until well combined and the nondairy butter is melted.

Drain the carrot chunks and place back in their saucepan. Add the corn kernels and the chipotle maple sauce. Stir, heat through, and serve.

8 ears of corn, shucked

3 carrots, peeled and sliced into 1-inch chunks

½ cup pure maple syrup

4 tablespoons nondairy butter

2 chipotle chiles in adobo sauce, finely chopped

1 teaspoon sea salt

¼ teaspoon freshly ground black pepper

Storing in the refrigerator:

This will keep in the refrigerator for up to 3 days. Heat in a saucepan or microwave before serving.

Freezing:

Let cool to room temperature. Freeze in freezer bags or hard-sided freezer containers for up to 3 months. To prepare after freezing, defrost in the refrigerator for 4 to 6 hours.

Reheating:

Heat through in a saucepan. You can also place in a microwave-safe bowl and microwave on high power for about 3 minutes, stirring every 45 seconds to check for heat.

Baked Stuffed Sweet Potatoes

Sweet potatoes are packed full of vitamins and minerals. These sweet potatoes are even better because they are packed with more veggies and then baked again. Great to have premade for when company is coming.

YIELD: 6 TO 8 SERVINGS | **ACTIVE TIME:** 25 MINUTES | **COOK TIME:** 45 MINUTES | **TOTAL TIME:** 1 HOUR 10 MINUTES

Preheat the oven to 350°F.

Wash and dry the sweet potatoes. Pierce with a fork so that they do not explode when baking. Place on a baking sheet and bake for 45 minutes. Pinch the center to test whether they are done. They should not be hard at all.

While the sweet potatoes are baking, heat the coconut oil in a large skillet over medium-high heat. Add the onion and mushrooms and sauté for 10 minutes. Add the beans and heat through for a couple of minutes.

Remove the baked sweet potatoes from the oven. Cut lengthwise right down the center so that you have two boat-shaped halves. Scoop out the center and place in a large bowl. Do this with all the sweet potatoes, reserving their shells.

Mash the sweet potatoes with a potato masher and add the nondairy butter, nondairy milk, salt, and pepper to taste. Mix well. Fold in the bean mixture. Taste to see whether you think it needs more salt or pepper.

Evenly divide the mixture among the empty sweet potato shells.

At this point you may refrigerate or freeze the stuffed potatoes; otherwise, place the potatoes on a baking sheet and bake for 20 minutes.

6 medium-size sweet potatoes, as oval as you can find

1 tablespoon coconut oil

½ cup red onion, diced

8 ounces button mushrooms, sliced

1 (15-ounce) can black beans, drained and rinsed

4 tablespoons nondairy butter

¼ cup nondairy milk

1 teaspoon sea salt

Freshly ground black pepper

1 tablespoon Nondairy Parmesan Cheese (page 131)

Storing in the refrigerator:

Place the stuffed potatoes in a large casserole dish and cover with plastic wrap. Store for up to 3 days.

Freezing:

Freeze in hard-sided freezer containers according to how many will fit comfortably in each container. Will keep for up to 4 months. Defrost in the refrigerator overnight. Some water may defrost into the dish but you can just drain this off and bake in a casserole or on a baking sheet as usual.

Baking or reheating after storing:

If refrigerated or frozen before baking, bake right in the casserole dish or on a baking sheet at 350°F for 25 to 30 minutes, or until the potatoes are hot all the way through.

If refrigerated after completely baking, microwave on high power for 1 minute, turn the potatoes 180 degrees and microwave on high power for another minute. Check the inside to make sure they are hot.

Cauliflower and Mushroom Crumble

Here is a recipe that makes it hard for you to put down your fork. The texture is perfect and you might be tempted to double the topping.

YIELD: 6 SERVINGS | **ACTIVE TIME:** 25 MINUTES | **COOK TIME:** 15 MINUTES | **TOTAL TIME:** 40 MINUTES

Place the florets in a medium-size saucepan and cover with water. Bring to a boil and cook for 5 minutes. Remove from the heat and drain. Place in a 9 x 9-inch baking dish (use a freezer-safe casserole if planning to freeze).

Heat the coconut oil in a large skillet over medium-high heat. Add the onion and mushrooms and sauté for 10 minutes. Spoon the mushroom mixture over the cauliflower.

In a small bowl, combine the nondairy butter, bread crumbs, Parmesan, nutritional yeast, parsley, salt, and pepper. Stir well. Sprinkle over the vegetables in the baking dish.

At this point you may refrigerate or freeze the casserole; otherwise preheat the oven to 350°F.

Bake for 15 minutes.

1 head cauliflower, cored and cut into florets

1 tablespoon coconut oil

½ cup white onion, chopped

8 ounces button mushroom, sliced

5⅓ tablespoons coconut oil

1 tablespoon nondairy butter, melted

1 cup vegan bread crumbs

½ cup Nondairy Parmesan Cheese (page 131)

1 tablespoon nutritional yeast

1 teaspoon dried parsley

1 teaspoon sea salt

¼ teaspoon freshly ground black pepper

NOTE:

A good way to cut florets is from the underside. First, core the cauliflower and cut close to the bottom of the florets. Break them apart into large bunches. Pick up one large bunch and on the underside, cut a small slit as if you were going to cut the cauliflower apart. Do not go all the way through; grasp the bunch with your fingers at the slit and pull apart from the underside. It goes very quickly. This lets the floret break at its natural split instead of making a hard knife cut. It is much prettier.

Storing in the refrigerator:

Will keep covered in the refrigerator for up to 3 days.

Freezing:

Cover the freezer-safe casserole with plastic wrap and then slide into a freezer bag. Will keep frozen for up to 3 months. To prepare after freezing, defrost in the refrigerator for 4 to 6 hours.

Baking after storing:

Bake in a 350°F oven for 20 minutes.

Italian Roasted Cauliflower

A little simplicity in your life is a good thing.

YIELD: 4 TO 6 SERVINGS | **ACTIVE TIME:** 15 MINUTES | **COOK TIME:** 30 MINUTES | **TOTAL TIME:** 45 MINUTES

Put everything into a large resealable plastic bag and shake well. Place the bag in a bowl. Let marinate in the refrigerator for 2 hours, turning the bag every half-hour.

Preheat the oven to 425°F.

Pour into a 9 x 9-inch baking dish. Bake for 25 to 30 minutes, stirring every 10 minutes. Serve hot.

1 head cauliflower, cut into florets

1 red bell pepper, cut into chunks

½ cup red onion, diced

1 cup of your favorite Italian dressing

1 tablespoon balsamic vinegar

1 tablespoon coconut oil

½ teaspoon sea salt

¼ teaspoon freshly ground black pepper

Storing in the refrigerator:

Drain the marinade off the vegetables and keep them covered in the refrigerator for up to 3 days.

Freezing:

Place the cooled roasted veggies in a freezer bag and keep frozen for up to 3 months. To prepare after freezing, defrost in the refrigerator for 2 to 4 hours.

Reheating:

Pour into a 9 x 9-inch baking dish.

If stored in the refrigerator, bake at 425°F for 25 minutes, stirring every 10 minutes.

If thawed from the freezer, bake at 350°F for 10 to 15 minutes.

Reheating:

If stored in the refrigerator, bake at 425°F for 25 minutes, stirring every 10 minutes.

If defrosted from the freezer, pour into a 9 x 13-inch baking dish. Bake at 350°F

Caramelized Vegetables

Roasting brings out a depth of flavor in vegetables that they can't get any other way. Caramelization then adds to the complexity. Top that off with this being a fast recipe and you have all the bases covered.

YIELD: 4 TO 6 SERVINGS | **ACTIVE TIME:** 15 MINUTES | **COOK TIME:** 30 MINUTES | **TOTAL TIME:** 45 MINUTES

In a large bowl, combine the nondairy butter, maple syrup, balsamic vinegar, and salt. Mix well.

Add the vegetables and toss until all are coated.

At this point you may refrigerate or freeze the vegetables; otherwise, preheat the oven to 425°F.

Pour the vegetables into a 9 x 13-inch baking dish. Bake for 25 minutes.

NOTE:

Before serving you can roast red potatoes separately and then toss them with the other roasted vegetables. There will be enough of the glaze to spread around the potatoes. Roasted potatoes become spongy and grainy when frozen, so I don't suggest freezing them with the original recipe.

4 tablespoons nondairy butter

¼ cup pure maple syrup

1 tablespoon plus 1 teaspoon balsamic vinegar

½ teaspoon salt

1 pound fresh green beans, snapped

1 small head cauliflower, cut into florets

4 carrots, sliced into 1-inch pieces

1 red onion, cut into thirds and then halved

Storing in the refrigerator:

Do not roast first. Pour into a 9 x 13-inch baking dish. Cover and keep in the refrigerator for up to 3 days. Bake at 425°F for 25 minutes, stirring every 10 minutes.

Freezing:

Place the cooled roasted veggies in a freezer bag and keep frozen for up to 3 months. To prepare after freezing, defrost in the refrigerator for 2 to 4 hours.

Vegan Sausage Dressing

A family favorite in any household, this sausage dressing can be served on holidays or as a satisfying side dish on any day. Stock up on packaged corn bread stuffing during the fall so that you can make it anytime during the year.

YIELD: 6 TO 8 SERVINGS | **ACTIVE TIME:** 30 MINUTES | **COOK TIME:** 30 MINUTES | **TOTAL TIME:** 1 HOUR

Lightly oil a 9 x 9-inch baking dish.

Melt 2 tablespoons of the nondairy butter in a large skillet over medium-low heat. Add the onion and sauté for 15 minutes, or until the onion becomes translucent.

Defrost the frozen sausage patties in the microwave on medium power for just a minute so that they can be crumbled in a food processor. Do not cook. Put the sausage in a food processor and process for just a few seconds to get crumbles.

Add the crumbled sausage to the onion. Add 1 more tablespoon of nondairy butter. Add the sage, Spike, salt, and pepper. Cook for 1 minute.

In a large bowl, combine the stuffing and the sausage mixture. Stir well. Add the vegetable stock and the remaining nondairy butter. Stir until well mixed.

At this point you may refrigerate or freeze the stuffing; otherwise, preheat the oven to 350°F.

Turn the mixture into the prepared baking dish. Cover with aluminum foil and bake for 30 minutes.

NOTE:

This freezes so well that you can make enough for occasional lunches for the next 4 months. Freeze in serving-size freezer containers. It doesn't even have to defrost. When you want a lunch, just microwave on high power for about a minute, stir, and lunch is served.

- ½ cup (1 stick, 4 ounces) nondairy butter, divided
- 1 cup yellow onion, finely diced or pulsed in a food processor
- 1 (8-ounce) box vegan sausage patties (6 patties)
- ½ teaspoon dried sage
- ½ teaspoon Spike seasoning blend
- 1 teaspoon salt
- ¼ teaspoon freshly ground black pepper
- 1¾ cups vegan vegetable stock
- 14 ounces vegan seasoned corn bread stuffing

Storing in the refrigerator:

You can keep the stuffing in the refrigerator for 2 to 3 days before or after baking.

Freezing:

Freeze before baking. Make sure the casserole is in a freezer-to-oven-safe casserole and covered tightly. It will keep in the freezer for up to 6 months. To prepare after freezing, defrost in the refrigerator for 4 to 6 hours.

Baking after storing:

Bake at 350°F for 35 minutes.

Slow Cooker Pull-Apart Pizza Rolls

The idea of pull-apart bread actually pulls a person in. Make it with pizza flavors and you just can't lose.

YIELD: 6 TO 8 SERVINGS | **ACTIVE TIME:** 15 MINUTES | **COOK TIME:** 1 HOUR 50 MINUTES | **TOTAL TIME:** 2 HOURS 5 MINUTES

In a small bowl, add the yeast to the warm water and stir well. Set aside.

In a stand mixer fitted with a paddle attachment, combine the nondairy milk, coconut oil, sugar, salt, and egg substitute. Beat at low speed to stir and pour in your yeast mixture. Let it stir until all is combined, scraping down the sides if necessary.

Change to a dough hook attachment and add the flour. Let mix on low speed for 6 to 8 minutes. The dough will be a little sticky but that should be okay. If you can't work with it, add a touch more flour. Pat into a ball and set aside.

Line a 6-quart slow cooker with parchment paper. I cut a larger circle so that it would go up the sides by about 3 inches. Then I snip vertically down the sides, all the way to the bottom, in about six places, so that the sides overlap and lay flat.

Place some of the pizza sauce in a bowl. Cut the ball of dough into 12 pieces. Roll each piece into a ball and use your fingers to roll pizza sauce all over the ball. Lay in the slow cooker, on the parchment paper, barely touching the sides. Continue with all the balls, to cover the bottom of the slow cooker in one layer. The balls may not touch in places but they will rise nicely and fill in any empty areas.

Cover and cook on LOW for 1 hour for rising. Then, turn the setting to HIGH and cook for 30 more minutes. Brush more sauce, lightly, on the tops of the rolls and cook another 20 minutes. Remove the rolls by grabbing the parchment paper by the sides and lifting. Let rest on a wire rack.

Serve warm or cold and with extra pizza sauce for dipping, if you like.

½ cup warm water (110°F)

2¼ teaspoons active dry yeast

½ cup nondairy milk

2 tablespoons coconut oil

2 teaspoons sugar

1 teaspoon sea salt

Vegan substitute for 1 egg, prepared

3 cups all-purpose flour, plus more if needed

½ cup pizza sauce

Storing in the refrigerator:

After cooling completely, store in a resealable plastic bag in the refrigerator for up to 1 week.

Freezing:

After cooling completely, freeze in a freezer bag for up to 3 months. To serve, defrost in the refrigerator for a few hours. The rolls are ready to eat anytime after defrosting.

Reheating:

After refrigerating or thawing, you may reheat the rolls on a baking sheet in a 350°F oven for 5 minutes.

CHAPTER FIVE

Hearty Meals

Slow Cooker Mushrooms and Rice

Have you heard of the slow cooker saying "dump and go"? This is exactly the type of recipe that is being referred to. All goes in the slow cooker at once, and you turn it on and go about your business. Perfect every time.

YIELD: 6 SERVINGS | **ACTIVE TIME:** 10 MINUTES | **COOK TIME:** 3 HOURS | **TOTAL TIME:** 3 HOURS 10 MINUTES

In the slow cooker, combine the rice, nondairy butter, onions, soup, 1 teaspoon of the salt, and the pepper. Mix well.

Lay the sliced mushrooms on top of the ingredients in the slow cooker. Push down lightly. This helps keep all the rice under the liquid and allows the mushrooms to cook at a bit of a slower pace.

Cook on LOW 6 to 8 hours or for 3 hours on HIGH.

Uncover and fluff to incorporate the mushrooms. Add up to 1 teaspoon of the remaining salt, to taste.

16 ounces uncooked long-grain rice

½ cup (1 stick, 4 ounces) nondairy butter, melted

2 medium-size onions, chopped

32 ounces vegan portobello soup (see note)

2 teaspoons salt (see note)

¼ teaspoon freshly ground black pepper

8 ounces button mushrooms, sliced

NOTES:

Alternatively, you can use your favorite vegan mushroom soup. If it is condensed, make at least 16 ounces of the soup, then add enough water or vegetable stock to make 32 ounces.

Although this soup seems to need the full 2 teaspoons of salt to balance the flavors, you may prefer to add only 1 teaspoon prior to cooking; taste and add more afterward, if desired.

Storing in the refrigerator:

After cooking and cooling, this will also keep in the refrigerator for up to 3 days.

Freezing:

After cooling, you can keep in the freezer in either freezer bags or hard-sided containers for up to 3 months. To prepare after freezing, defrost in the refrigerator for 3 to 4 hours.

Reheating:

Place in a microwave-safe bowl and microwave on high power for 3 minutes, stirring every 45 seconds. Check that it is hot enough.

Rigatoni and Vegan Sausage Casserole

Rigatoni with a red sauce sounds good to start with, but add some animal-free protein and you have a main course.

YIELD: 8 SERVINGS | **ACTIVE TIME:** 20 MINUTES | **COOK TIME:** 40 MINUTES | **TOTAL TIME:** 1 HOUR

Lightly grease a 9 x 13-inch casserole with coconut oil.

Cook the pasta according to the package directions and set aside.

Chop the vegan sausage into small pieces and set aside.

In a large skillet, heat the coconut oil over medium-high heat. Add the onion and mushrooms and sauté for 15 minutes. Add the garlic and cook for another 2 minutes, stirring so as to not burn the garlic.

Add the wine and oregano and bring to a boil. Cook until the liquid is reduced by about half. Add the tomatoes, tomato sauce, vegetable stock, and sausage. Bring to a boil again, then lower the heat, cover, and simmer for 15 minutes.

You should have about 1½ cups of sauce. Spread about ½ cup of the sauce in the bottom of the prepared casserole. Divide the remaining sauce into two equal portions. Pour the pasta into ½ cup of the reserved sauce and mix. Pour the pasta mixture into the casserole. Cover with the last ½ cup of reserved sauce.

At this point you may refrigerate or freeze the casserole; otherwise preheat the oven to 350°F.

Cover the casserole with a casserole lid or foil. Bake for 20 minutes. Uncover and bake for another 10 minutes.

1 tablespoon coconut oil, plus more for casserole

12 ounces whole wheat rigatoni pasta

1 (10-ounce) package vegan Italian sausage

½ cup white onion, chopped

8 ounces button mushrooms

2 cloves garlic, finely chopped

¾ cup dry red wine, such as zinfandel or merlot

1 teaspoon dried oregano

1 (14-ounce) can stewed tomatoes

1 (8-ounce) can tomato sauce

½ cup vegan vegetable stock

Storing in the refrigerator:

The casserole will keep in the refrigerator before and after baking for up to 3 days each.

Freezing:

Freeze before the casserole is baked. Make sure it is in a freezer-safe casserole with a freezer-safe snap lid. You may also use two smaller freezer-to-oven-safe casseroles and then slide them into freezer bags. Will keep for up to 4 months. To prepare after freezing, defrost in the refrigerator overnight.

Baking after storing:
Bake in a 350°F oven, covered, for 20 minutes. Uncover and bake for another 10 minutes.

Cooking after storage:

Place in a microwave-safe bowl. Microwave on high power for 2 minutes, stirring after 1 minute and every 20 seconds after that, checking for heat. Serve on your favorite taco shells with avocado and lettuce.

Black Bean Salsa Tacos

Here is a fresh twist for taco night. There are lots of spices added to a traditional salsa and then amped up with veggies. You can serve it either hot or cold.

YIELD: 4 SERVINGS | **ACTIVE TIME:** 15 MINUTES | **COOK TIME:** 2 MINUTES | **TOTAL TIME:** 17 MINUTES

Put all the ingredients in a microwave-safe bowl and mix well. Let marinate for 1 hour in the refrigerator.
The salsa may be refrigerated or frozen at this point.

Place in the microwave and cook on HIGH for 2 minutes, stirring after a minute and every 20 seconds after that, checking for heat.

Serve on your favorite taco shells with avocado and lettuce.

1 chipotle chile in adobo sauce, finely chopped

2 tablespoons salsa

1 tablespoon balsamic vinegar

1 tablespoon fresh lime juice

1 tablespoon coconut oil

1 (15-ounce) can black beans, drained and rinsed

1 ear of corn, kernels cut off the cob

½ cup red onion, finely diced

½ teaspoon ground cumin

½ teaspoon raw sugar

½ teaspoon sea salt

½ teaspoon freshly ground black pepper

Storing in the refrigerator:

The salsa will keep in the refrigerator before heating for up to 5 days and after heating for up to 3 days.

Freezing:

Freeze the salsa in a hard-sided freezer-safe container for up to 3 months. To prepare after freezing, defrost in the refrigerator overnight.

Lasagne Rolls

A simple twist on lasagna has the addition of a creamy cashew cheese rolled up inside. This creates a wonderful casserole and if you add a big salad, your meal is complete.

YIELD: 6 SERVINGS | **ACTIVE TIME:** 30 MINUTES | **COOK TIME:** 30 MINUTES | **TOTAL TIME:** 1 HOUR

In a large skillet, heat the coconut oil over medium-high heat. When the oil is hot, add the mushrooms and cook for 10 minutes. Set aside.

Cook the lasagna noodles al dente, according to the package directions. Set aside.

To assemble the rolls: Spread 1½ cups of marinara sauce in the bottom of a 9 x 13-inch casserole dish.

Lay one noodle lengthwise on the counter in front of you. Spread about 2 tablespoons of the cashew cheese down the center. Add about six mushroom slices, zigzag style, down the center of the cashew cheese. Next, snap any hard stems off the spinach leaves and lay the leaves over the mushrooms, overlapping each other by a little bit.

Roll the lasagna noodle upward, evenly and tightly. Set the roll, seam side down, in the prepared casserole. Repeat the steps until all the noodles are used.

Spread the rest of the cashew cheese sauce and marinara over the top of the rolled noodles. Mix the cheese and sauce and smooth out with the back of a tablespoon. At this point you may refrigerate or freeze the lasagna rolls; otherwise, preheat the oven to 350°F.

Bake for 25 to 30 minutes.

1 tablespoon coconut oil

8 ounces portobello mushrooms, sliced

2 cups Cashew Cheese (recipe follows)

12 lasagna noodles

32 ounces Slow Cooker Marinara Sauce (page 231)

8 ounces baby spinach

Cashew Cheese

2 cups raw cashews, soaked for 2 hours to overnight

4 cloves garlic

1 tablespoon fresh lemon juice

1 tablespoon Dijon mustard

¾ cup vegan vegetable stock

1 cup nutritional yeast

½ teaspoon onion powder

1 teaspoon sea salt

¼ teaspoon freshly ground black pepper

Drain the soaked cashews.

Place the garlic in a food processor. Process until finely chopped. Place everything in the food processor and process until smooth. You will need to scrape down the sides of a bowl with a spatula every once in a while.

Storing in the refrigerator:

The casserole will keep in the refrigerator before and after baking for up to 3 days each.

Freezing:

Freeze before the casserole is baked. Make sure it is in a freezer-safe casserole with a freezer-safe snap lid. You may also use two smaller freezer-to-oven-safe casseroles and then slide them into freezer bags. Will keep in the freezer for up to 6 months. To prepare after freezing, defrost in the refrigerator overnight.

Baking after storage:

Bake in a 350°F oven, covered, for 25 minutes. Uncover and bake for another 10 minutes.

Teriyaki Stir-Fry

Stir-fries are fast and fun. This rendition has snow peas, which adds a nice sweetness to the teriyaki.

YIELD: 4 SERVINGS | **ACTIVE TIME:** 15 MINUTES | **COOK TIME:** 15 MINUTES | **TOTAL TIME:** 30 MINUTES

Have everything prepped and ready to cook. The veggies may be refrigerated or frozen at this point.

Heat the coconut oil in a wok or large skillet over medium-high heat.

When the oil is hot, add the bell peppers, onion, and mushrooms. Toss and stir and continue doing this movement for about 5 minutes. As you continue to stir, add the snow peas, teriyaki sauce, and pepper. Continue to cook, stirring and tossing, for 2 minutes. Great served over rice.

- 2 tablespoons coconut oil
- 1 red bell pepper, seeded and cut into long strips
- 1 yellow bell pepper, seeded and cut into long strips
- ½ cup red onion, thinly sliced
- 1 cup button mushrooms
- 8 ounces snow peas
- ½ cup vegan teriyaki sauce
- ¼ teaspoon freshly ground black pepper

Storing in the refrigerator:

The freshly prepared vegetables will keep in the refrigerator before and after cooking for up to 3 days each.

Freezing:

Freeze the vegetables in a freezer bag or in a hard-sided freezer-safe container for up to 3 months. To prepare after freezing, defrost in the refrigerator for 3 to 4 hours.

Cooking after storing:

Cook in coconut oil as directed.

Cowboy Lasagne

Layers of lasagna noodles are interspersed with black beans, corn, and so much more. Southwestern comfort food to the max.

YIELD: 6 SERVINGS | **ACTIVE TIME:** 30 MINUTES | **COOK TIME:** 25 MINUTES | **TOTAL TIME:** 55 MINUTES

Heat the coconut oil in a large skillet over medium-high heat. When it is hot, add the vegan beef and heat through, reducing it to crumbles. Remove from the pan and set aside.

Add the onion and mushrooms to the skillet and sauté for 10 to 15 minutes, until the onion is translucent. Return the beef to the pan. Add the black olives, 20 ounces of the tomatoes, and the corn, black beans, oregano, thyme, salt, and pepper. Mix well and heat through.

Meanwhile, cook the lasagna noodles al dente, according to the package directions. Set aside.

To assemble the lasagna: Spread the remaining 8 ounces of the tomatoes in the bottom of a casserole. Reserve 1 cup of the vegan beef sauce. Lay three of the noodles on the bottom of the casserole to cover completely. Spread 1½ cups of the sauce over that layer. Dot ⅓ cup of the cashew cheese across the sauce. Lay three more noodles and spread another 1½ cups of sauce over that layer. Dot another ⅓ cup of cashew cheese on that layer. Lay the last three noodles and spread the remaining (not the reserved) sauce over the top. Dot the remaining ⅓ cup of cashew cheese on the top and use the back of a tablespoon to combine and spread the reserved sauce and cheese all over the top.

At this point you may refrigerate or freeze the casserole; otherwise, preheat the oven to 350°F.

Bake for 25 minutes.

NOTE:

Use an egg slicer to slice your olives about three or four at a time. It goes very quickly.

9 lasagna noodles, cooked according to the package directions

1 tablespoon coconut oil

1 (10-ounce) package vegan ground beef

½ cup white onion, diced

8 ounces button mushrooms

1 (8-ounce) can black olives, drained and sliced

1 (28-ounce) can fire-roasted tomatoes, divided

1 (14-ounce) can organic corn, drained and rinsed

1 (14-ounce) can black beans, drained and rinsed

½ teaspoon dried oregano

½ teaspoon dried thyme

1 teaspoon salt

¼ teaspoon freshly ground black pepper

1 cup Cashew Cheese (page 179)

Storing in the refrigerator:

The casserole will keep in the refrigerator before and after baking for up to 3 days each.

Baking after storing:

Bake in a 350°F oven, covered, for 25 minutes. Uncover and bake for another 10 minutes.

Freezing:

Freeze before the casserole is baked. Make sure it is in a freezer-safe casserole with a freezer-safe snap lid. You may also use two smaller freezer-to-oven-safe casseroles and then slide them into freezer bags. It will keep for up to 4 months. To prepare after freezing, defrost in the refrigerator overnight.

South of the Border Black Beans and Rice

Black beans and rice is a comfort food special to South of the Border. Add just a squeeze of lime juice over the top.

YIELD: 6 SERVINGS | **ACTIVE TIME:** 20 MINUTES | **COOK TIME:** 6 HOURS | **TOTAL TIME:** 6 HOURS 20 MINUTES

Do not soak the black beans. Pick through the beans to make sure there are no pebbles. Put the beans in a slow cooker.

Add the vegetable stock, 1 cup of water, and the onion, hot sauce, cumin, salt, and baking soda. Stir well.

Cover and cook on LOW for 6 to 8 hours. If you want it faster, you can cook on HIGH for 3 to 4 hours. The liquid will dissipate quicker on HIGH, so watch the liquid level.

Check about halfway through and see whether the beans have absorbed most of the liquid. If it seems too dry, add warm to hot water in ½-cup increments.

Serve with rice. Optional toppings can be tomatoes, onion, and lime wedges. Very traditional.

16 ounces dried black beans

32 ounces vegan vegetable stock

1 cup water

1 very small white onion, chopped

1 teaspoon hot sauce

2 teaspoons ground cumin

1 teaspoon sea salt

½ teaspoon baking soda
(to soften the beans)

1¾ cup warm to hot water,
if necessary

Storing in the refrigerator:

The beans will keep in the refrigerator after cooking for up to 3 days.

Freezing:

Freeze in hard-sided freezer-safe containers for 3 to 4 months. To prepare after freezing, defrost in the refrigerator overnight.

Reheating:

Heat in the microwave on high power or over medium heat in a saucepan. Serve with brown rice.

American Tetrazzini

This is a recipe that is used at our house, a lot, when company is coming. It is frozen before you bake it and when it is removed from the oven the hot creamy casserole is very inviting.

YIELD: 6 SERVINGS | **ACTIVE TIME:** 30 MINUTES | **COOK TIME:** 25 MINUTES | **TOTAL TIME:** 55 MINUTES

Preheat the oven to 350°F. Lightly grease a 9 x 13-inch casserole dish with the coconut oil. If you are going to freeze the casserole, grease two smaller freezer-safe casserole dishes that have freezer-safe lids.

To make the tetrazzini sauce: Cover the cashews with water and let soak for 4 hours to overnight. Drain the cashews and put into a food processor.

To the food processor, add the nondairy milk, nutritional yeast, garlic powder, salt, and pepper. Process until smooth. Taste for seasoning and add more salt or pepper, if you like. Set aside.

Bring a large pot of water to a boil for the spaghetti. Add the salt.

Break the uncooked spaghetti into thirds. To do this, take about a third of the package of spaghetti and hold it over a large bowl. Grasp with both hands about a third up the bunch and snap, then snap the remaining two-thirds of the bunch in half. Do this with all the spaghetti. Add to the salted boiling water.

Cook al dente, according to the package directions, probably 7 to 8 minutes. Drain and place back in the empty pot.

Pour the tetrazzini sauce into the pot. Stir well. Pour this mixture into the prepared casserole dish. At this point you may refrigerate or freeze the casserole; otherwise, preheat the oven to 350°F.

Cover the casserole with foil and bake for 25 minutes.

FOR THE TETRAZZINI SAUCE:

1 tablespoon coconut oil

1 cup cashews

1¼ cups nondairy milk

1 tablespoon nutritional yeast

1 teaspoon garlic powder

1 teaspoon salt

¼ teaspoon freshly ground black pepper

10 ounces spaghetti pasta

2 tablespoons salt, for the boiling water

Storing in the refrigerator:

The casserole will keep in the refrigerator before and after baking for up to 3 days each.

Freezing:

Freeze before the casserole is baked. Make sure it is in a freezer-safe casserole with a freezer-safe snap lid. You may also use two smaller freezer-to-oven-safe casseroles and then slide them into freezer bags. Will keep for up to 4 months. To prepare after freezing, defrost in the refrigerator overnight.

Baking after storage:

Bake in a 350°F oven, covered with foil, for 20 minutes. Uncover and bake for another 10 minutes.

Storing in the refrigerator:

The filling will keep in the refrigerator for up to 3 days.

Freezing:

Freeze the filling only in freezer-safe containers with hard sides and a tight lid. Will keep for up to 6 months. To serve after freezing, defrost in the refrigerator overnight.

Reheating:

Microwave on high power for 15 seconds just to take the chill off. Serve as described.

Ranch Tacos

Tacos are so popular they have actually been associated with a day of the week. The spicy coolness of homemade ranch dressing will make you want this taco recipe every single Taco Tuesday.

YIELD: 10 TACOS | **ACTIVE TIME:** 25 MINUTES | **COOK TIME:** 5 MINUTES | **TOTAL TIME:** 30 MINUTES

To make the ranch dressing: Put the soaked cashews in a food processor. Add all the remaining dressing ingredients. Process until smooth. Add more nondairy milk, if needed, to get the consistency of dressing.

The flavors will meld after resting in the refrigerator for a couple of hours, but you can still use it immediately.

Pour into a container and store in the refrigerator. The dressing will keep in the refrigerator for about 2 weeks.

To make the tacos: Steam the cauliflower florets for 15 minutes. Let cool and break up into very small pieces. Place in a large bowl.

Add the chickpeas, tomato, hot sauce, salt, and pepper. Mix well.

If you have soft tacos, fry them in hot oil for a minute or two on each side. Fold over to drain and cool in a taco shape. If you are using hard tacos, you are ready to go.

To assemble: Spoon the filling into each taco, add baby spinach, and drizzle with ranch dressing. Serve.

FOR THE RANCH DRESSING:

1 cup cashews, soaked for at least 4 hours or overnight

¾ cup nondairy milk, plus more if needed

3 tablespoons cider vinegar

1 tablespoon pure maple syrup

2 teaspoons onion powder

½ teaspoon dried parsley

½ teaspoon dried chives

½ teaspoon dried dill

½ teaspoon freshly ground black pepper

FOR THE TACOS:

1 head cauliflower, cut into florets

1 (15-ounce) can chickpeas, drained and rinsed

1 tomato, diced

1 teaspoon hot sauce

½ teaspoon sea salt

¼ teaspoon freshly ground black pepper

10 vegan corn tortillas of your choice, hard or soft

Oil, for frying (optional)

Baby spinach, rinsed well

Dill

Californian Chili and Rice Casserole

Rice is such a great staple and it can be turned into just about any regional dish. Chili is a good match and for this recipe I have updated an old favorite.

YIELD: 6 SERVINGS | **ACTIVE TIME:** 25 MINUTES | **COOK TIME:** 25 MINUTES | **TOTAL TIME:** 50 MINUTES

In a large skillet, heat the coconut oil over medium-high heat. When the oil is hot, add the onion and bell pepper and cook for about 10 minutes, until the onion is translucent. Add the garlic and cook, stirring, for 2 more minutes.

Stir in the tomatoes, rice, pinto beans, cashew mayonnaise, chili powder, and salt. Heat through for a few minutes.

Pour the rice mixture into a 2-quart casserole. It will be shallow, which will give more of a surface to spread the corn chips. Do not add the corn chips yet.

At this point you may refrigerate or freeze the casserole; otherwise, preheat the oven to 350°F.

Bake for 20 minutes. Sprinkle the corn chips over the top and bake for another 5 minutes.

1 tablespoon coconut oil

½ cup white onion, diced

1 small green bell pepper, chopped

1 clove garlic, finely diced

1 (14.5-ounce) can fire-roasted tomatoes

2 cups cooked rice

1 (15-ounce) can pinto beans, drained and rinsed

⅔ cup Cashew Mayonnaise (recipe follows)

1 teaspoon chili powder

½ teaspoon sea salt

2 cups smashed vegan corn chips

Cashew Mayonnaise

¾ cup cashews

½ cup water

2 tablespoons fresh lemon juice, plus more if desired

½ teaspoon dry mustard

½ teaspoon sea salt

¼ teaspoon freshly ground black pepper

¼ cup olive oil, plus more if desired (see note)

Soak the cashews overnight or at least 4 hours. They will bulk up in size. Drain.

Place the cashews in a blender. Add the rest of the ingredients, except the oil.

Blend at medium speed until the mixture is as smooth as you can get it. Different blenders will do different

work because of the amount of power that they have. No matter what your blender, you will get a delicious cashew mayonnaise.

Now, slowly pour in the olive oil through the opening in the lid. I found ¼ cup to be perfect but you may add a little more if you would like it thinner.

Taste the mixture. See whether you would like a little bit more lemon juice. Sometimes I do, but not always.

NOTE:

Coconut oil will get very hard in the refrigerator, so olive oil is best.

Storing in the refrigerator:

The casserole will keep in the refrigerator before and after baking for up to 3 days each.

Freezing:

Freeze before the casserole is baked. Do not add the corn chips before freezing. Make sure it is in a freezer-safe casserole with a freezer-safe snap lid. You may also use two smaller freezer-to-oven-safe casseroles and then slide them into freezer bags. Will keep for up to 6 months. To prepare after freezing, defrost in the refrigerator overnight. Stir before using.

Baking after storing:

Bake at 350°F for 25 minutes. Sprinkle the corn chips over the top and bake for another 5 minutes.

Red Lentil and Rice Loaf

It is nice to have options, and you have many with this nourishing loaf. You can have it sliced for supper with your favorite sauce or you can have it on nutty bread as a sandwich.

YIELD: 6 SERVINGS | **ACTIVE TIME:** 15 MINUTES | **COOK TIME:** 1 HOUR 15 MINUTES | **TOTAL TIME:** 1½ HOURS

Lightly grease a 9 x 5-inch loaf pan with coconut oil.

Pick through the lentils to make sure there are no pebbles. Rinse and drain.

In a large saucepan, bring the lentils and vegetable stock to a boil. Lower the temperature and simmer for 15 minutes. Drain. Lightly mash the lentils so that only about half are mashed.

In a small skillet, heat the coconut oil over medium-high heat. Add the onion and sauté for 10 minutes. Add the garlic and sauté for 2 more minutes.

Add the onion mixture, rice, oats, salt, barbecue sauce, sage, and oregano to the lentils. Mix well.

Transfer the mixture to the prepared loaf pan and spread out evenly. At this point you may refrigerate or freeze the loaf; otherwise, preheat the oven to 350°F.

Bake for 1 hour. To serve, dot a little barbecue sauce on the top and with some on the side.

1 tablespoon coconut oil, plus more for pan

1¼ cups dried red lentils

3 cups vegan vegetable stock

½ cup white onion, diced

2 cloves garlic, finely chopped

2 cups cooked brown rice

1 cup quick-cooking oats

1 teaspoon sea salt

¼ cup vegan barbecue sauce, plus more for serving

½ teaspoon ground sage

½ teaspoon dried oregano

Storing in the refrigerator:

The baked lentil loaf will keep in the refrigerator for up to 3 days.

Freezing:

Freeze in a freezer-safe container or freezer bag for up to 6 months. You may also use two smaller freezer-to-oven safe casseroles and then slide them into freezer bags.

Reheating:

To reheat after freezing, cut into thick slices and microwave on medium or high power for 4 to 5 minutes, rotating and flipping the slices every minute.

Slow Cooker Black-Eyed Peas

Black-eyed peas are a traditional dish to have on New Year's Day. It is said to bring good luck on every day for each legume that you eat. The leftovers are as good as they are on the first day.

YIELD: 6 SERVINGS | **ACTIVE TIME:** 15 MINUTES | **COOK TIME:** 6 HOURS | **TOTAL TIME:** 6 HOURS 15 MINUTES

The night before cooking: Pick through the beans to make sure there are no pebbles. Put the beans in a large bowl and cover with water to clean. Swish your hand around in the water and pick out any beans that don't look good or that float. Drain the beans.

Place the beans in a very large pot or bowl. Add fresh water to cover the beans by about 3 inches. Let soak on the counter overnight. They will plump up.

The morning of cooking: Drain the beans and put them in a slow cooker. Add the vegetable stock, onion, garlic, herbs, and salt and pepper. Add enough water to just cover the beans.

Cook on LOW for 6 to 8 hours. Alternatively, the beans can also be cooked on HIGH for 3 to 4 hours. Give a bean a pinch at the end of cooking to make sure they are the softness that you like. Or . . . have a spoonful.

16 ounces dried black-eyed peas

2 cups vegan vegetable stock

1 small onion, diced

1 clove garlic, finely diced

1 bay leaf

⅛ teaspoon dried thyme

¼ teaspoon ground sage

1 teaspoon salt

½ teaspoon freshly ground black pepper

About 2 cups water

Storing in the refrigerator:

The black-eyed peas will keep in the refrigerator for up to 3 days.

Freezing:

After cooling, freeze in a freezer-safe container with hard sides and a tight lid for up to 6 months. To serve after freezing, defrost in the refrigerator overnight because it is a pretty solid mass and will take longer to thaw.

Reheating:

Place in a saucepan and heat through. You could also reheat in a microwave.

Bay leaf

Five-Spice Comfort Pita Sandwiches

Sandwiches translate to comfort food. The rice and mushrooms play off each other wonderfully in this recipe. Especially when they are linked with tamari and crunchy cabbage slaw.

YIELD: 6 SANDWICHES | **ACTIVE TIME:** 10 MINUTES | **COOK TIME:** 15 MINUTES | **TOTAL TIME:** 25 MINUTES

Heat the coconut oil over medium-high heat in a large skillet or wok.

Add the mushrooms and cook for 10 minutes. Add the carrot, if using, red bell pepper, and five-spice and cook for 2 minutes.

Add the tamari, rice, and red onion and heat through.

Cut the pita pockets in half and stuff with the rice mixture along with the shredded cabbage and baby spinach.

1 tablespoon coconut oil

8 ounces button mushrooms, sliced

1 carrot, julienned (if using slaw mix, you can omit this)

½ red bell pepper, diced

2 teaspoons Chinese five-spice powder

3 tablespoons tamari

4 cups cooked brown rice

¼ cup red onion, diced

6 pita pockets

Shredded cabbage or slaw mix

Baby spinach

Storing in the refrigerator:

The sandwich filling will keep in the refrigerator up to 3 days. Assemble the sandwiches at the time of serving.

Freezing:

Freeze the filling only in a freezer bag or hard-sided container. The filling will keep for up to 3 months. Defrost for a couple of hours in the refrigerator.

Reheating:

Microwave on high power for 2 minutes, stirring and checking for heat every 30 seconds.

Just Right Sweet Potato Patties

This is a big batch of patties. Make for a party or for freezing, so that you have easier preparation for a few meals in the future.

YIELD: 16 PATTIES | **ACTIVE TIME:** 45 MINUTES | **COOK TIME:** 1 HOUR | **TOTAL TIME:** 1 HOUR 45 MINUTES

Preheat the oven to 400°F.

Wash the sweet potatoes and poke with a knife to help to vent the stream when cooking. Bake for 45 to 50 minutes. Carefully squeeze the sweet potatoes at the end of cooking to make sure they give a bit and are cooked all the way through. If not, cook at 5-minute increments.

Put the corn in a large bowl. Add the black beans, chipotle and adobo sauce, oats, cumin, garlic powder, and salt. Mix well, mashing the beans with a fork as you go.

Scoop out the sweet potatoes and place the flesh in the bowl along with the other ingredients, except the coconut oil. Mix well. Form the mixture into about 16 patty shapes. At this point you may freeze the patties.

Otherwise, heat the coconut oil in a skillet and cook two patties at a time, about 10 minutes on each side, until crispy. This helps the patties to stay together. Serve as a side dish or as a sandwich.

4 large sweet potatoes (about 1 pound each)

4 ears of corn, kernels cut off the cob

1 (15-ounce) can black beans, drained and rinsed

4 chipotle chiles in adobo sauce, finely chopped, and about 2 tablespoons adobo sauce from the can

2 cups rolled oats

2 teaspoons ground cumin

1 teaspoon garlic powder

2 teaspoon sea salt

1 tablespoon coconut oil, for frying

Freezing:

If freezing some or all before frying, wrap each patty individually in plastic wrap. Stack the wrapped patties into a freezer bag. They will keep for up to 3 months. To prepare, take how many patties you desire out of the freezer and defrost in the refrigerator for an hour or so. They do not have to be completely defrosted before frying.

Frying after freezing:

Fry in hot oil as directed.

Frying after freezing:
Fry in hot oil as directed.

Chipotle Lentil Patties

A great way to use up leftover lentils, but you can also use canned lentils as this recipe calls for. This recipe is so good you might want to stock up.

YIELD: 8 PATTIES | **ACTIVE TIME:** 20 MINUTES | **COOK TIME:** 15 MINUTES | **TOTAL TIME:** 35 MINUTES

Heat the olive oil in a skillet over medium-high heat. Add the onion and sauté for 10 minutes. Add the garlic and cook for another 2 minutes, watching so as not to burn the garlic.

Clean the cauliflower and break into florets. Steam for 15 minutes. Combine the cauliflower and drained lentils in a large bowl and mash with the tines of a fork. Add the remaining ingredients, except the coconut oil. Mix very well.

Form into eight patties. Press the patties together hard, so they will keep together. At this point you may freeze the patties.

Otherwise, heat the coconut oil in a skillet and cook two patties at a time for 8 minutes on one side, flip and cook 7 more minutes. Do not press down on the patties when you are frying them. This is one of the culprits that makes bean burgers fall apart. You are actually separating the ingredients when you press down.

1 teaspoon olive oil

½ cup white onion, diced

2 cloves garlic, diced small

1 very small head cauliflower (to equal volume of lentils)

2 (15-ounce) cans lentils, drained and rinsed

1 carrot, grated

¼ cup finely chopped almonds

1 cup vegan bread crumbs

1 chipotle chile in adobo sauce, seeds removed

2 teaspoons cider vinegar

1 teaspoon dried parsley

½ teaspoon sea salt

1 tablespoon coconut oil, for frying

Storing in the refrigerator:

The patties will keep in the refrigerator for up to 2 days before frying or up to 3 days after frying.

Freezing:

If freezing some or all, place on a baking sheet as you are forming the patties. Freeze for 1 hour. Remove the patties with a spatula and wrap individually in plastic wrap, then slide them all into a freezer bag. They will keep for up to 3 months. When ready to prepare, defrost in the refrigerator f or about 3 hours.

Panini Chili Bean Cakes

These versatile patties can be served alone as a main dish or made into a sandwich. You could use any sauce that you like and they also go really well with avocado slices.

YIELD: 15 BEAN CAKES | **ACTIVE TIME:** 20 MINUTES | **COOK TIME:** 20 MINUTES | **TOTAL TIME:** 40 MINUTES

Heat the coconut oil in a skillet over medium-high heat. Add the onion and sauté for 10 minutes. Lower the heat to low. Add the carrot, chili powder, and cumin. Cook for another 5 minutes.

Place the beans in a large bowl and mash with a potato masher or the tines of a large fork. Add the Dijon mustard, sunflower seeds, oats, tomato paste, salt, pepper, and the onion mixture. Mix well.

Form 15 patties. At this point you may refrigerate or freeze the bean cakes.

Otherwise, heat a panini pan that has ridges as if for grilling. Lightly oil the pan with a silicone brush. Place two cakes at a time in the prepared pan. Close the lid and let the cakes cook for about 8 minutes.

1 tablespoon coconut oil

½ cup white onion, finely diced

2 cloves garlic, finely diced

½ cup grated carrot

1½ teaspoons chili powder

1 teaspoon ground cumin

2 (15-ounce) cans kidney beans, drained and rinsed

1 tablespoon Dijon mustard

½ cup hull-less sunflower seeds

½ cup rolled oats

2 tablespoons tomato paste

1 teaspoon sea salt

¼ teaspoon freshly ground black pepper

Oil, for panini pan

Storing in the refrigerator:

The bean cakes will keep in the refrigerator for up to 2 days before frying or up to 3 days after frying.

Freezing:

If freezing some or all, place on a baking sheet as you form the cakes. Freeze for 1 hour. Remove the patties with a spatula and wrap individually in plastic wrap, then slide them all into a freezer bag. The cakes will keep up to 3 months in the freezer. When ready to prepare, defrost in the refrigerator for about 3 hours.

Cooking after storage:
Cook on a lightly oiled panini press.

Baking after storing:

Bake in a 350°F oven for 30 minutes.

Black Beans and Rice Enchiladas

Beans and rice makes this a more substantial casserole. The tortillas are rolled around a slew of ingredients and then baked with a rich and spicy enchilada sauce.

YIELD: 12 ENCHILADAS | **ACTIVE TIME:** 20 MINUTES | **COOK TIME:** 1 HOUR 10 MINUTES | **TOTAL TIME:** 1½ HOURS

In a skillet that has a lid, heat the coconut oil over medium-high heat. Add the onion and cook for 10 minutes. Add the rice and stir for a couple of minutes. Add the salsa, vegetable stock, cumin, chili powder, and salt. Bring to a boil, cover, then reduce the heat to a simmer. Cook for about 40 minutes, until the rice is done. Check at 30 and 35 minutes.

Add the beans and tomato and heat through.

Have ready a 9 x 13-inch casserole dish.

Pour the enchilada sauce into a 9 x 9-inch baking dish so that you can dip each tortilla into the sauce.

Dunk a tortilla into the sauce and then lay in the 9 x 13-inch casserole. Spoon about ⅓ cup of the bean mixture down the center of the tortilla and roll up in the casserole. Push to one edge of the casserole. Continue with the remaining tortillas until the casserole dish is full. Pour the remaining enchilada sauce over the top of the rolled enchiladas. Sprinkle with the Cheddar.

At this point you may refrigerate or freeze the casserole; otherwise, preheat the oven to 350°F.

Bake for 30 minutes.

1 tablespoon coconut oil
½ cup white onion, diced
1 cup uncooked brown rice
1 cup of your favorite salsa
2 cups vegan vegetable stock
½ teaspoon ground cumin
½ teaspoon chili powder
¼ teaspoon sea salt
1 (15-ounce) can black beans, drained and rinsed
1 tomato, cored, seeded, and diced
1 (28-ounce) can enchilada sauce
12 whole wheat tortillas
8 ounces nondairy Cheddar cheese

Storing in the refrigerator:

The casserole will keep in the refrigerator before and after baking for up to 3 days each.

Freezing:

Freeze before the casserole is baked. Make sure it is in a freezer-safe casserole with a freezer-safe snap lid. You may also use two smaller freezer-to-oven-safe casseroles and then slide them into freezer bags. This casserole will keep for up to 3 months in the freezer. To prepare after freezing, defrost in the refrigerator overnight.

Vegetable Enchiladas

Who doesn't like Mexican-style food? There is so much flavor! These tortillas are packed with unusual vegetables that will keep you smiling at how good they taste.

YIELD: 6 SERVINGS | **ACTIVE TIME:** 30 MINUTES | **COOK TIME:** 30 MINUTES | **TOTAL TIME:** 1 HOUR

Preheat the oven to 300°F.

In a medium-size bowl, toss the sweet potatoes in 1 tablespoon of the coconut oil. Spread out on a baking sheet. Bake at 300°F for 20 minutes, or until they can be pierced easily with a fork.

Heat the remaining tablespoon of oil in a skillet over medium-high heat. When hot, add the onion and mushrooms and sauté for 10 minutes. Add the chili powder and cumin and cook for another minute. Add the corn kernels, red bell peppers, black beans, and rice. Heat through for about 5 minutes.

Have ready a 9 x 13-inch casserole dish.

Pour the enchilada sauce into a 9 x 9-inch baking dish so that you can dip each tortilla into the sauce.

Dunk a tortilla into the sauce and then lay in the 9 x 13-inch casserole. Spoon about ⅓ cup of sauce down the center of the tortilla and roll up in the casserole. Push to one edge of the dish. Continue with the remaining tortillas until the casserole dish is full. Pour the remaining enchilada sauce over the top of the rolled enchiladas.

At this point you may refrigerate or freeze the casserole; otherwise, preheat the oven to 350°F.

Bake for 30 minutes.

1 pound sweet potatoes, peeled and diced into ½-inch pieces

2 tablespoons coconut oil, divided

½ cup white onion, diced

16 ounces button mushrooms, sliced

2 teaspoons chili powder

½ teaspoon ground cumin

½ cup frozen corn, thawed

2 roasted red bell peppers (about 1 cup)

1 (15-ounce) can black beans, drained and rinsed

1 cup cooked short-grain brown rice

1 (16-ounce) can enchilada sauce

10 vegan whole wheat tortillas

Storing in the refrigerator:

The casserole will keep in the refrigerator before and after baking for up to 3 days each.

Freezing:

Freeze before the casserole is baked. Make sure it is in a freezer-safe casserole with a freezer-safe snap lid. You may also use two smaller freezer-to-oven-safe casseroles and then slide them into freezer bags. This will keep for up to 3 months in the freezer. To prepare after freezing, defrost in the refrigerator overnight.

Baking after storage:

Bake in a 350°F oven for 30 minutes.

Frying after storage:

Microwave the edamame mixture on high power for a few minutes, stirring every 30 seconds, and serve over freshly fried polenta.

Edamame and Lentils over Fried Polenta

Polenta is an overlooked choice for meals. This recipe takes advantage of the store-bought tube that is easily sliced and fried. Cover it with the unique edamame topping for complete enjoyment.

YIELD: 6 SERVINGS | **ACTIVE TIME:** 20 MINUTES | **COOK TIME:** 15 MINUTES | **TOTAL TIME:** 35 MINUTES

Pick through the lentils to make sure there are no pebbles. Rinse and place in a large saucepan. Add enough vegetable stock to just cover the lentils. Bring to a boil, then lower the heat to a low boil, low enough that you can barely see the lentils moving. Add more stock a little at a time if it starts to get below the lentil level. Cook for 25 to 30 minutes. Do not overcook.

Cook the edamame according to the package directions. Drain.

Drain the lentils and return them to the saucepan. Add the edamame, garam masala, salt, and pepper. Cook over medium heat for 5 minutes.

At this point you may refrigerate or freeze the edamame mixture. Otherwise, heat the coconut oil in a skillet. Slice the polenta about ¾-inch thick and fry on both sides. Serve the lentil mixture over the polenta with a little tomato and red onion sprinkled over the top.

1 cup dried brown lentils

14 ounces vegan vegetable stock

6 ounces frozen, shelled edamame

1 teaspoon garam masala

1 teaspoon sea salt

¼ teaspoon freshly ground black pepper

2 tablespoons coconut oil

1 (16-ounce) tube refrigerated polenta

2 small Roma tomatoes, diced small, for garnish

½ cup red onion, diced small, for garnish

Storing in the refrigerator:

The edamame mixture will keep in the refrigerator for up to 3 days.

Freezing:

Don't freeze the fried polenta. Go ahead and eat any leftover fried polenta with maple syrup or dip it in marinara sauce. After cooling, freeze the edamame mixture in a freezer-safe container with hard sides and a tight lid. This will keep for up to 3 months in the freezer. To prepare after freezing, defrost in the refrigerator for a couple of hours.

Vegetable Curry

Curry dishes are very popular and with good reason. The spices are bold and the sauce is creamy. Team that up with loads of veggies and rice for a great meal.

YIELD: 8 SERVINGS | **ACTIVE TIME:** 20 MINUTES | **COOK TIME:** 15 MINUTES | **TOTAL TIME:** 35 MINUTES

In a large stockpot, heat the coconut oil over medium-high heat. Add the onion and sauté for 10 minutes. Add the garlic and cook for another minute. Add the garam masala and cayenne. Stir for a few seconds to cook the spices.

Add the tomato paste and mix in. Add the vegetable stock and coconut milk. Cook on high heat, stirring, and bring to a boil. Lower the heat and simmer for 10 minutes.

Add the cauliflower, tomatoes, and carrots. Bring to a boil over medium-high heat. Cover and lower the heat to a simmer. Cook for 20 minutes.

Add the chickpeas and salt and heat through, 3 to 5 minutes. Serve with rice.

2 tablespoons coconut oil

1 small yellow onion, diced

4 medium garlic cloves, minced

2 teaspoons garam masala

½ teaspoon cayenne pepper

1 tablespoon tomato paste

2 cups vegan vegetable stock

1 cup canned pure coconut milk (do not use coconut beverages)

1 small head cauliflower, cut into very small florets

2 tomatoes, cored, seeded, and diced

2 carrots, peeled and cut into ½-inch slices

1 (15-ounce) can chickpeas, drained and rinsed

½ teaspoon sea salt

Storing in the refrigerator:

The vegetable curry will keep in the refrigerator for 3 days.

Freezing:

After cooling, freeze in a freezer-safe container with hard sides and a tight lid for up to 3 months in the freezer. To prepare after freezing, defrost in the refrigerator overnight.

Reheating:

Place in a saucepan and heat through, or heat in the microwave.

Reheating:

Microwave the sauce, lightly
covered with a paper towel,
on high power for 2 minutes,
stirring every 30 seconds.

Pizza Sandwiches

This is a delicious sandwich that has layers of sautéed veggies and the tangy flavors of a pizza sauce. A casual sandwich that comes together easily on any day of the year.

YIELD: 4 SANDWICHES | **ACTIVE TIME:** 20 MINUTES | **COOK TIME:** 15 MINUTES | **TOTAL TIME:** 35 MINUTES

To make the sauce: Place the oil in a small saucepan and add the garlic. Over medium heat, cook for 1 to 2 minutes. Watch so that you don't burn the garlic; it cooks fast.

Stir in the tomato paste, sugar, oregano, and salt. Cook over medium-high heat, stirring often, for 2 to 3 minutes, until the tomato sauce starts to bubble. Remove from the heat. At this point you may refrigerate or freeze the sauce.

To make the sandwiches: Heat the coconut oil in a large skillet over medium-high heat. Add the onion and sauté for 10 to 15 minutes, or until the onion is translucent. Set aside.

Add both bell peppers to the pan and sauté for about 15 minutes until they are soft and tender. Remove from the pan.

Add the mushrooms to the pan and sauté them for about 15 minutes, until they cook some of their liquid out. Remove from the pan.

Assemble the sandwiches: Spread a layer of pizza sauce on a slice of bread and then keep adding layers of the grilled vegetables, topped with greens. Put more sauce on the bread top and then slice in half for easier handling.

FOR THE SAUCE:

4 tablespoons extra-virgin olive oil

4 cloves garlic, very finely diced

12 ounces tomato paste

2 teaspoons sugar

1 teaspoon dried oregano

1 teaspoon sea salt

FOR THE SANDWICHES:

1 tablespoon coconut oil, for grilling

¼ red onion, sliced into rings

1 red bell pepper, sliced into long strips

1 yellow bell pepper, sliced into long strips

8 ounces cremini mushrooms, sliced

8 slices of your favorite sandwich bread

Mixed greens, for sandwich topping

Storing in the refrigerator:

The pizza sauce will keep for up to 4 days in the refrigerator. The grilled veggies will keep for 3 to 4 days. For reheating the veggies just heat through in a frying pan to freshen up.

Freezing:

After cooling, pack the sauce into little freezer jars or hard-sided freezer containers. It will keep for up to 4 months. To prepare after freezing, defrost the sauce in the refrigerator overnight.

White Bean Sandwiches

If you've never had a white bean sandwich, now is your chance. Go ahead and pile on the beans and have a bite. Now, that's good!

YIELD: 8 SANDWICHES | **ACTIVE TIME:** 15 MINUTES | **COOK TIME:** 1 HOUR 20 MINUTES | **TOTAL TIME:** 1 HOUR 35 MINUTES

Pick through the navy beans to make sure there are no pebbles. Rinse. Soak overnight, covered by at least 2 inches of water. The beans will swell. Drain the beans.

Pour the beans into a large soup pot. Add the vegetable stock and bring to a boil. Lower the heat and simmer over medium heat. Add the bay leaves.

In a saucepan, heat the coconut oil over medium-high heat. When it is hot, add the onion. Sauté for about 10 minutes. Add the garlic and cook for a couple more minutes. Add the onion mixture to the beans.

Add the cumin and cloves to the bean mixture. Cover and cook over medium heat, stirring occasionally, for about 1½ hours. Take off the cover the last half-hour and let the extra liquid cook away.

Stir in the salt, pepper, lemon juice, and hot sauce.

Spread on your favorite sandwich bread. It goes great with watercress and/or baby spinach. Red onion goes well, too. More hot sauce, anyone?

16 ounces dried navy beans

32 ounces vegan vegetable stock

2 bay leaves

1 tablespoon coconut oil

¼ cup white onion, diced small

2 cloves garlic, finely chopped

1 teaspoon ground cumin

¼ teaspoon ground cloves

1 teaspoon sea salt

Pinch of freshly ground black pepper

2 teaspoons fresh lemon juice

Dash of hot sauce

Storing in the refrigerator:

Will keep covered in the refrigerator for 2 to 3 days.

Freezing:

Let cool to room temperature. Freeze in hard-sided freezer containers for up to 3 months. To prepare after freezing, defrost in the refrigerator overnight.

Reheating:

Heat on high power for a minute in the microwave just to bring it closest to room temperature.

Pasta Chili Bake

It is always a good thing when two favorites can be blended into one recipe. Chili and pasta are the two favorites I am talking about. The best of both worlds.

YIELD: 6 TO 8 SERVINGS | **ACTIVE TIME:** 20 MINUTES | **COOK TIME:** 25 MINUTES | **TOTAL TIME:** 45 MINUTES

Cook the penne pasta al dente, according to the package directions. Drain and set aside in a large bowl.

In a large skillet, heat the coconut oil over medium-high heat. Add the onion and sauté for 10 minutes. Add the vegan beef, chili powder, tomatoes, and salsa. Cook, stirring well, for 5 minutes.

Pour the sauce over the pasta in the large bowl. Mix well.

Pour into a 9 x 13-inch baking dish. Sprinkle the cheese over the top. At this point you may refrigerate or freeze the casserole; otherwise, preheat the oven to 350°F.

Bake for 25 minutes.

10 ounces penne pasta

1 tablespoon coconut oil

½ cup white onion, diced

1 (10- to 12-ounce) package vegan ground beef

2 tablespoons chili powder

4 large Roma tomatoes, diced

1 cup salsa

8 ounces mixed grated nondairy cheese, white and Cheddar

Storing in the refrigerator:

You may prepare this casserole ahead, but do not bake it. It will keep in the refrigerator for up to 2 days.

Freezing:

You may prepare this casserole ahead, but do not bake it. Pack the casserole in a freezer-safe casserole that can also go in the oven. It will keep for up to 3 months in the freezer. To prepare after freezing, defrost in the refrigerator overnight.

Baking after storage:

Bake at 350°F for 25 minutes.

Roasted Veggies Bowl

Perfectly cooked vegetables are roasted and seasoned for a good balance. The Cheesy Almond Sauce makes the meal fresh and new in style.

YIELD: 4 SERVINGS | **ACTIVE TIME:** 30 MINUTES | **COOK TIME:** 30 MINUTES | **TOTAL TIME:** 1 HOUR

Preheat the oven to 400°F.

Sprinkle the coconut oil on a baking sheet. Arrange the cauliflower, broccoli, and chickpeas onto the baking sheet. Toss to coat the vegetables with the oil. Sprinkle with salt and pepper.

Roast for 30 minutes, tossing the vegetables after 15 minutes.

Remove from the oven.

Toss with the red onion and cashews. Serve with Cheesy Almond Sauce.

1 tablespoon coconut oil

1 head cauliflower, cleaned and cut into florets

1 head broccoli, cleaned and cut into florets

1 (15-ounce) can chickpeas, drained, rinsed, and patted dry with a paper towel

½ teaspoon sea salt

¼ teaspoon freshly ground black pepper

½ cup red onion, diced

½ cup cashews

Cheesy Almond Sauce (recipe follows)

Cheesy Almond Sauce

¾ cup raw almonds, soaked for 8 hours or overnight

½ cup water

¼ cup nutritional yeast

2 tablespoons fresh lemon juice (about ½ lemon), plus more if desired

½ teaspoon dry mustard

½ teaspoon sea salt

¼ teaspoon freshly ground black pepper

½ cup olive oil, plus more if desired

Pure maple syrup (optional)

Drain the almonds and place in a blender.

Add the rest of the ingredients, except the oil and maple syrup.

Blend at medium-high speed until the mixture is as smooth as you can get it. Different blenders will do different work because of the amount of power that they have. No matter what your blender, you will get a delicious almond sauce.

Now, slowly pour in the olive oil through the opening in the lid. I found ½ cup to be perfect, but you may add a little more if you would like it thinner.

Taste the sauce. See whether you would like a little bit more lemon juice. Sometimes I do, but not always. Some people like a dash of maple syrup, also.

This will keep in the fridge for about 1 week. It would get too solid if you used coconut oil, so olive oil is best. This does not freeze, so if 1½ cups is too much, you can cut the ingredients in half.

Storing in the refrigerator:

All the veggies can be prepared, but not cooked, and kept in the refrigerator for up to 4 days. Prepare as directed above.

Freezing:

After baking, let cool completely. Freeze separately from the sauce in freezer bags or hard-sided containers. It will keep in freezer for up to 3 months.

CHAPTER SIX

Extra Embellishments

Homemade Ketchup

Here is a delicious ketchup that you can make year-round even when you don't have fresh tomatoes in the garden. You will become a kid again and want to put this it on everything.

YIELD: 1³/4 CUPS KETCHUP | **ACTIVE TIME:** 15 MINUTES | **COOK TIME:** 0 | **TOTAL TIME:** 15 MINUTES

Mix all the ingredients together and it is done.

1 (12-ounce) can tomato paste

½ cup cider vinegar

½ cup water

1 teaspoon pure maple syrup

½ teaspoon sea salt

1 teaspoon dried oregano

½ teaspoon dry mustard

¼ teaspoon garlic powder

⅛ teaspoon ground ginger

⅛ teaspoon ground nutmeg

⅛ teaspoon freshly ground black pepper

Storing in the refrigerator:

Will keep in the refrigerator for about 3 weeks.

Freezing:

Freeze in ½-pint freezer jars or in ice cube trays as tablespoon-size servings. After the tablespoon-size servings are frozen, transfer them to a freezer bag. The ketchup will keep in the freezer for 5 to 6 months.

Basil Nut Pesto

It is the little things that make a recipe special. Basil Nut Pesto is one of those little things. It is very easy to make and it can be frozen by the tablespoon for just a dash of flavoring, or by the half-pint for a future sauce or casserole.

YIELD: 1 CUP PESTO | **ACTIVE TIME:** 5 MINUTES | **COOK TIME:** 10 MINUTES | **TOTAL TIME:** 15 MINUTES

Preheat the oven to 350°F.

Place the walnuts on a baking sheet and toast in the oven for 10 minutes. Let cool.

Put the walnuts, basil leaves, and garlic in a food processor. Process until almost smooth. Slowly add the olive oil while processing.

Pour into a bowl and stir in the nutritional yeast, salt, and pepper.

¼ cup walnuts

4 cups fresh basil leaves (4 ounces)

3 cloves garlic

2 tablespoons olive oil

1 tablespoon nutritional yeast

¼ teaspoon sea salt

Pinch of freshly ground black pepper

Storing in the refrigerator:

Will keep in the refrigerator for 5 to 7 days.

Freezing:

Freeze in ½-pint freezer jars or in ice cube trays as tablespoon-size servings. After the tablespoon-size servings are frozen, transfer them to a freezer bag. The pesto will keep in the freezer for 3 to 4 months.

Roasted Tomatillo Salsa

Let's get real with a true Mexican-style salsa that is cherished as a necessary condiment.

YIELD: 1½ CUPS SALSA | **ACTIVE TIME:** 10 MINUTES | **COOK TIME:** 15 MINUTES | **TOTAL TIME:** 25 MINUTES

Preheat the oven to 475°F.

Put the coconut oil on a baking sheet and then add the tomatillos, garlic, and jalapeño. Toss in the oil. Roast for 15 minutes.

Remove from the oven and add everything to a food processor. Pulse until well blended. Serve with burritos, tacos, and even as a dip.

NOTE:
While removing the jalapeño seeds, wear rubber gloves and do not touch your face.

1 tablespoon coconut oil

1 pound tomatillos, husked

4 cloves garlic, peeled

1 jalapeño pepper, seeded (see note)

¾ cup pitted black olives

¾ cup fresh cilantro

2 tablespoons fresh lime juice

¾ teaspoon sugar

½ teaspoon sea salt

2 tablespoons water

Storing in the refrigerator:

Let cool and store in ½-pint glass jars. Will keep in the refrigerator for 2 weeks.

Freezing:

Freeze in ½-pint freezer jars for up to 6 months. Defrost in the refrigerator.

Thai Sweet Chili Sauce

A traditional Asian sauce is always good to have on hand. Thai Sweet Chili Sauce is a great one because it is so versatile. You can even mix a little into cooked brown rice. You will have a treat.

YIELD: 2 CUPS SAUCE | **ACTIVE TIME:** 10 MINUTES | **COOK TIME:** 6 MINUTES | **TOTAL TIME:** 16 MINUTES

Place all the ingredients, except the potato starch and the 2 tablespoons of water, in a blender. Blend at medium speed until smooth. The pepper and garlic will be in small bits.

Pour into a small saucepan and bring to a boil. Lower the heat and simmer for 3 to 5 minutes.

Meanwhile, in a small bowl, mix the potato starch and 2 tablespoons of water. Stir well. Add to the pepper mixture. Simmer for another minute. The sauce will thicken.

2 red jalapeño chiles, seeded (see note)

3 cloves garlic, peeled

¼ cup white vinegar

½ teaspoon red hot sauce

½ cup sugar

¾ cup plus 2 tablespoons water, divided

1 teaspoon sea salt

1 tablespoon potato starch (you may use cornstarch)

NOTE:

While removing the jalapeño seeds, wear rubber gloves and do not touch your face.

Storing in the refrigerator:

Let cool and store in ½-pint glass jars. This seems to keep forever but a month is best.

Freezing:

Freeze in ½-pint freezer jars for 5 to 6 months. Defrost in the refrigerator.

Slow Cooker Marinara Sauce

A marinara sauce that is spiced just right can't be beat. The fact that you can make it and take advantage of a slow cooker at the same time is a real prize.

YIELD: 5 CUPS SAUCE | **ACTIVE TIME:** 15 MINUTES | **COOK TIME:** 8 HOURS | **TOTAL TIME:** 8 HOURS 15 MINUTES

Put all the ingredients into a slow cooker. Cook on LOW for 8 hours. Remove the bay leaves and stir.

Serve hot or let cool for storing.

1 (28-ounce) can diced tomatoes

1 (6-ounce) can tomato paste

1 tablespoon pure maple syrup

1 tablespoon balsamic vinegar

½ cup water

1 small white onion, diced

1 teaspoon garlic powder

2 bay leaves

1 tablespoon dried basil

1 teaspoon dried oregano

½ teaspoon salt

¼ teaspoon freshly ground black pepper

Storing in the refrigerator:
Will keep in the refrigerator for 3 to 4 days.

Freezing:
Freeze in 1-pint freezer jars for 5 to 6 months.

Slow Cooker Vegetable Spaghetti Sauce

When you are looking for a red sauce with more oomph to the bite, this loaded vegetable sauce is the one to make.

YIELD: 4 CUPS SAUCE | **ACTIVE TIME:** 15 MINUTES | **COOK TIME:** 7 HOURS | **TOTAL TIME:** 7 HOURS 15 MINUTES

In a large skillet, heat the coconut oil over medium-high heat. Add the onion and carrot. Cook for 5 minutes. Transfer to a slow cooker.

Add the remaining ingredients. Stir well. Cook on LOW for 7 to 8 hours.

Serve hot or let cool for storing.

1 tablespoon coconut oil

½ cup white onion, diced

1 carrot, diced

8 ounces button mushrooms, sliced thickly

1 green bell pepper, diced

2 (14-ounce) cans diced tomatoes

1 (6-ounce) can tomato paste

2 teaspoons pure maple syrup

1 teaspoon Italian seasoning

½ teaspoon sea salt

¼ teaspoon freshly ground black pepper

Storing in the refrigerator:

Will keep in the refrigerator for 3 to 4 days.

Freezing:

Freeze in 1-pint freezer jars for 5 to 6 months.

Blueberry Ginger Preserves

Sweet fruity blueberry jam is perfect to smear on toast and it is equally awesome to pile on a couple of scoops of nondairy vanilla ice cream.

YIELD: 2 CUPS PRESERVES | **ACTIVE TIME:** 5 MINUTES | **COOK TIME:** 30 MINUTES | **TOTAL TIME:** 35 MINUTES

Place all the ingredients in a medium-size saucepan. Bring to a boil over medium-high heat. Keep at a low boil and cook the mixture down for about 30 minutes.

Remove from the heat and let cool.

2 cups frozen blueberries

2 tablespoons pure maple syrup

1 tablespoon hemp seeds

1 tablespoon fresh ginger, peeled and grated

1 tablespoon fresh lemon juice

Ginger

Storing in the refrigerator:

Will keep in the refrigerator for 5 to 7 days.

Freezing:

Freeze in ½- to 1-pint freezer jars for up to 6 months.

extra embellishments

Strawberry Chia Jam

Deliberate simplicity, and chia seeds boost this jam's protein power with one little scoop.

YIELD: 2 CUPS JAM | **ACTIVE TIME:** 5 MINUTES | **COOK TIME:** 15 MINUTES | **TOTAL TIME:** 20 MINUTES

Chop the strawberries into small pieces or process with a couple of pulses in a food processor.

Place the strawberries in a medium-size saucepan over medium-high heat. Add the maple syrup. Slowly bring to a boil and cook at a low boil for about 10 minutes.

Add the chia seeds and cook for another 5 minutes. Remove from the heat and let cool. The jam will continue to thicken as it sits.

16 ounces fresh strawberries, hulled and rinsed

¼ cup pure maple syrup

1 tablespoon chia seeds

Storing in the refrigerator:

Will keep in the refrigerator for 2 to 3 weeks.

Freezing:

Freeze in 1-pint freezer jars for up to 6 months. Defrost in the refrigerator. After defrosting the jam will keep in the refrigerator for 2 to 3 weeks.

Butterscotch Sauce

This butterscotch sauce is rich, thick, and creamy, which is perfect for pouring over nondairy ice cream. Try not to eat it with a spoon because it will be gone too fast.

YIELD: 2 CUPS SAUCE | **ACTIVE TIME:** 5 MINUTES | **COOK TIME:** 15 MINUTES | **TOTAL TIME:** 20 MINUTES

In a medium-size saucepan over medium heat, melt the nondairy butter. Add the brown sugar and coconut cream. Stir well.

Bring the mixture to a high simmer and let cook for 4 to 5 minutes. Do not stir during this process.

Remove from the heat and let cool for about 10 minutes, then stir in the vanilla and salt. Serve warm over any vegan ice cream or coffee cake.

4 tablespoons nondairy butter

1 cup light brown sugar

½ cup plus 2 tablespoons full-fat coconut cream (17% to 22% fat)

½ teaspoon vanilla extract

¼ teaspoon sea salt

Storing in the refrigerator:

Store in a covered jar, in the refrigerator, for 3 weeks.

Freezing:

Freeze in ½-pint freezer jars for up to 6 months. Defrost in the refrigerator.

Reheat:

To serve, microwave on high power for just seconds. Stir to make sure it is defrosted and if not, microwave on high power for a few more seconds.

Praline Sauce

The richness of this praline sauce brings up the thought of one word. Decadence. Perfect over vegan ice cream, bread pudding, and pumpkin pie.

YIELD: 2 CUPS SAUCE | **ACTIVE TIME:** 10 MINUTES | **COOK TIME:** 5 MINUTES | **TOTAL TIME:** 15 MINUTES

In a small saucepan, combine the brown sugar, evaporated nondairy milk, and nondairy butter. Cook, stirring, over low heat for about 5 minutes. Remove from the heat and add the vanilla and pecans. Serve warm.

2½ cups light brown sugar

12 ounces Nondairy Slow Cooker Evaporated Milk (recipe follows)

2 tablespoons nondairy butter

1 teaspoon vanilla extract

½ cup chopped pecans

Nondairy Slow Cooker Evaporated Milk

1⅓ cups water, plus more if needed

1 cup dairy-free soy powder

I have come up with the timing and measurements that will give you a 12-ounce "can" when it is all done.

Place the water and soy milk powder in a slow cooker. Stir well.

Do NOT cover because it has to cook down to become evaporated milk.

Cook on HIGH for 1½ hours.

Pour in a measuring cup to make sure you have 12 ounces. (I say to do this because some slow cookers might cook a little bit hotter. If it has evaporated too much, you can add a little bit more water to get the measurement correct.)

Storing in the refrigerator:

Store in a covered jar, in the refrigerator, for 3 weeks.

Freezing:

Freeze in ½-pint freezer jars for up to 6 months. Defrost in the refrigerator.

Reheat:

To serve, microwave on high power for just seconds. Stir to make sure it is defrosted and if not, microwave on high power for a few more seconds.

CHAPTER SEVEN

Sweetness

Chocolate Crêpes

With a small pan and a twist of the wrist, you will have chocolate crepes. Roll them up all by themselves for a snack or top with your favorite jam for a decadent treat.

YIELD: 12 CREPES | **ACTIVE TIME:** 10 MINUTES | **COOK TIME:** 15 MINUTES | **TOTAL TIME:** 25 MINUTES

In a large bowl, combine all of the ingredients, except the coconut oil. Mix with an electric mixer on low speed until the mixture is completely blended. Put in the refrigerator to rest for an hour. When ready to make your crepes, take the batter out of the refrigerator and stir by hand.

Heat a drop of coconut oil in small skillet over medium-high heat. Pour a scant ¼ cup of the batter. Lift the pan and swirl and tilt to cause the batter to cover the bottom. Cook for about 2 minutes, until golden brown, then flip and cook for a minute more. Remove from the pan and continue with the rest of the batter, adding a drop of coconut oil to the pan every once in a while. They cook best without much oil.

Serve folded over, filled with strawberry or blueberry jam. A chocolate hazelnut spread is great, too.

½ cup nondairy milk

½ cup water

¼ cup plus 2 tablespoons pure maple syrup

1 cup all-purpose flour

¼ cup unsweetened cocoa powder

½ teaspoon baking powder

¼ teaspoon sea salt

Coconut oil, for frying

Storing in the refrigerator:

Will keep in the refrigerator for up to 1 week.

Freezing:

Freeze in freezer bags and just take out a few when you want. They defrost almost immediately. Will keep in the freezer for 3 to 4 months.

Chocolate Matcha Mint Cookies

Completely vegan and delicious, but darn those cookies. Maybe we would like less sugar and fat, so don't overindulge.

YIELD: 30 COOKIES | **ACTIVE TIME:** 30 MINUTES | **COOK TIME:** 10 MINUTES | **TOTAL TIME:** 40 MINUTES

Preheat the oven to 350°F. Line a couple of baking sheets with parchment paper.

In a medium-size bowl, mix together the flours, cocoa powder, baking powder, and salt.

In a large bowl, mix together the maple syrup, nondairy milk, egg substitute, and vanilla.

Add the dry ingredients to the wet ingredients about ½ cup at a time.

Using a cookie scoop that is about 1 inch across, scoop out the dough and place about 2 inches apart on the prepared baking sheet. Lightly press down the top of each dough ball. You want them a little fat and they don't spread too much.

Bake for 8 to 10 minutes. Let cool on a wire rack for 10 minutes.

Fill with the mint filling, or freeze and fill just before serving.

1 cup whole wheat flour

1 cup all-purpose flour

½ cup unsweetened cocoa powder

1 teaspoon baking powder

½ teaspoon sea salt

¾ cup pure maple syrup

¼ cup nondairy milk

Vegan substitute for 1 egg, prepared

1 teaspoon vanilla extract

Mint Filling (recipe follows)

Mint

Mint Filling

4 cups powdered sugar

2 cups (4 sticks, 1 pound) nondairy butter, at room temperature

2 teaspoons vanilla extract

½ teaspoon peppermint extract

1 teaspoon matcha (for the soft green coloring)

Mix all the ingredients together by hand or with an electric mixer on medium speed.

Spoon some filling into a piping bag fitted with a fat round tip. Flip half of the cookies over so that the flatter side is up. Pipe a dollop of the filling into the center of each cookie.

Place another cookie on top of the filling and lightly press down.

Storing in the refrigerator:

Will keep in the refrigerator for 4 to 5 days.

Freezing:

The cookies are freezable before filling and I would make the frosting fresh.

They defrost almost immediately. Will keep in the freezer for 3 to 5 months.

Cinnamon Maple Cookies

Cinnamon maple is a perfect combination and when the flavors get turned into cookies, eyes will roll in ecstasy. These are big cookies so get your munch on.

YIELD: 36 COOKIES | **ACTIVE TIME:** 20 MINUTES | **COOK TIME:** 10 MINUTES | **TOTAL TIME:** 30 MINUTES

Preheat the oven to 350°F. Lightly grease a baking sheet with the coconut oil.

In a bowl, combine the flours, baking soda, and salt. Set aside.

Mix the ground cinnamon and sugar together and set aside also.

In a large bowl, with an electric mixer, beat the shortening on medium speed until light and fluffy. Slowly add the maple syrup and beat until it is well incorporated. Beat in the vanilla.

Add the flour mixture to the maple syrup mixture and mix until just combined. Fold in the pecans.

Drop by heaping tablespoons, 2 inches apart, on the prepared baking sheet. Flatten a bit and sprinkle with the cinnamon-sugar. Bake for 8 to 10 minutes. Remove from the oven and place the cookies on wire racks to cool.

1 tablespoon coconut oil

1 cup all-purpose flour

½ cup whole wheat flour

1 teaspoon baking powder

1 teaspoon sea salt

2 teaspoons ground cinnamon

3 tablespoons sugar

1 cup vegan shortening

1 cup pure maple syrup

1 teaspoon vanilla extract

1 cup pecans

Storing in the refrigerator:

Will keep in the refrigerator for 4 to 5 days.

Freezing:

Freeze in freezer bags and just take out a few when you want. They defrost almost immediately. Will keep in the freezer for up to 5 months.

Big Fat Cherry Pecan Cookies

No complaints here. The title says it all, and they are perfectly mild sweet cookies.

YIELD: 36 COOKIES | **ACTIVE TIME:** 20 MINUTES | **COOK TIME:** 10 MINUTES | **TOTAL TIME:** 30 MINUTES

Preheat the oven to 350°F. Lightly grease baking sheets with the coconut oil.

In a large bowl, cream the butter and sugars until light and fluffy. Add the egg substitute to the mixture. Mix well.

In another bowl, mix together the flours, baking powder, and salt. Add to the sugar mixture and mix until combined.

Fold in the chocolate chips, cherries, and pecans.

Drop by rounded tablespoonfuls onto the prepared baking sheet. Bake for 10 minutes. Remove from the oven and cool for a couple of minutes, then transfer them to a wire rack to cool completely.

1 tablespoon coconut oil

1 cup (2 sticks, 8 ounces) nondairy butter, at room temperature

½ cup granulated sugar

½ cup packed light brown sugar

Vegan substitute for 1 egg, prepared

1¾ cups all-purpose flour

½ cup whole wheat flour

1 teaspoon baking powder

½ teaspoon sea salt

2 cups vegan semisweet chocolate chips

1 cup dried cherries, chopped

1 cup pecans, chopped

Storing in the refrigerator:

Will keep in the refrigerator for 1 week.

Freezing:

Freeze in freezer bags and just take out a few when you want. They defrost almost immediately. Will keep in the freezer for up to 5 months.

Chocolate Sugar Cookies

Chocolate is a game changer. A cookie here and there is a special treat that everyone deserves, so why not make it a chocolate one.

YIELD: 36 COOKIES | **ACTIVE TIME:** 20 MINUTES | **COOK TIME:** 9 MINUTES | **TOTAL TIME:** 29 MINUTES

Preheat the oven to 350°F. Line two baking sheets with parchment paper. Place the granulated sugar in a dish.

In a large bowl, combine the flours, cocoa powder, and baking soda. Mix and set aside.

In a large bowl, combine the brown sugar, melted nondairy butter, vanilla, and salt. Mix with an electric mixer on medium speed until it is well mixed. Add the mashed banana and mix until smooth.

Add the flour mixture and mix until just combined. Divide into 36 balls and roll each ball in the granulated sugar. Place about 2 inches apart on the prepared baking sheets. Flatten each ball with the bottom of a glass to about 2 inches wide.

Bake one baking sheet at a time for 9 minutes. Remove from the oven and let cool for 5 minutes, then transfer the cookies to a wire rack to cool completely.

¼ cup granulated sugar

1 cup all-purpose flour

1½ cups whole wheat flour

½ cup unsweetened cocoa powder

½ teaspoon baking soda

1¾ cups packed dark brown sugar

14 tablespoons (1 stick plus 6 tablespoons, 7 ounces) nondairy butter, melted and cooled a bit

1 teaspoon vanilla extract

½ teaspoon salt

1 banana, mashed

Storing in the refrigerator:

Will keep in the refrigerator for 4 to 5 days.

Freezing:

Freeze in freezer bags and just take out a few when you want. They defrost almost immediately. Will keep in the freezer for up to 5 months.

Magic Cookie Bars

This is a very fun recipe to make. It is an old standard that I have modernized and veganized. Everything is layered right in the baking pan and then baked.

YIELD: 24 BARS | **ACTIVE TIME:** 20 MINUTES | **COOK TIME:** 25 MINUTES | **TOTAL TIME:** 45 MINUTES

Preheat the oven to 350°F.

Pour the melted nondairy butter in a 9 x 13-inch baking pan. Sprinkle the graham cracker crumbs evenly over the melted nondairy butter.

Sprinkle the chopped nuts over the crumbs. Scatter the chocolate chips over the nuts. Sprinkle the coconut over the chocolate chips.

Evenly drizzle the sweetened condensed nondairy milk over the top. It will cover the whole thing. If small spots are missed, that is okay. You can't spread the topping, so drizzling is important.

Bake for 25 minutes. Let cool in the pan for 15 minutes. Cut into bars.

½ cup (1 stick, 4 ounces) nondairy butter, melted

1½ cups vegan graham cracker crumbs

1 cup walnuts, chopped

1 cup vegan semisweet chocolate chips

1⅓ cups unsweetened shredded coconut

14 ounces Sweetened Condensed Nondairy Milk (recipe follows)

Sweetened Condensed Nondairy Milk

YIELD: 14 OUNCES NONDAIRY MILK | **ACTIVE TIME:** 5 MINUTES
COOK TIME: 1 HOUR 30 MINUTES | **TOTAL TIME:** 1 HOUR 35 MINUTES

1½ cups nondairy milk, plus more if needed

3 tablespoons nondairy butter

½ cup coconut sugar (or you can use granulated sugar)

1 teaspoon vanilla extract

Place the nondairy milk, nondairy butter, and coconut sugar in a slow cooker. Stir well.

Do NOT cover because it has to cook down to become condensed.

Cook on HIGH for 1½ hours. Stir about every 30 minutes.

Add the vanilla and stir. Pour in a measuring cup to make sure you have 14 ounces. (I say to do this because some slow cookers might cook a little bit hotter. If it has condensed too much you can add a little bit more milk to get the measurement correct.)

Storing in the refrigerator:
Will keep in the refrigerator for 1 week.

Freezing:
Freeze in freezer bags and just take one or more when you get the craving. They defrost almost immediately. Will keep in the freezer for up to 4 months.

Peanut Butter Chocolate Crunch Bars

Ultimate satisfaction abounds when you take a bite of these soft and crunchy peanut butter bars. The fresh peanuts inside really add to the quality.

YIELD: 24 BARS | **ACTIVE TIME:** 20 MINUTES | **COOK TIME:** 25 MINUTES | **TOTAL TIME:** 45 MINUTES

Preheat the oven to 350°F. Lay a piece of foil across and over two opposite edges of a 9 x 13-inch baking pan. This will help you remove the bars from the pan.

In a medium-size bowl, mix together the flours, baking soda, and salt.

In a large bowl, combine the melted nondairy butter and the sugars. Beat with an electric mixer on medium speed until well mixed and smooth. Beat in the egg substitute, peanut butter, and vanilla. Beat well.

Add the flour and mix by hand until just combined. Fold in the chocolate chips and peanuts.

Turn into the prepared baking pan, smoothing out the top. Bake for 25 minutes. Remove from the oven and let cool on a wire rack. Lift with the foil overhanging "handles" and place on a cutting board. Cut into 24 bars.

1¾ cups all-purpose flour

½ cup whole wheat flour

½ teaspoon baking powder

½ teaspoon sea salt

12 tablespoons (1½ sticks, 6 ounces) nondairy butter, melted

¾ cup packed light brown sugar

½ cup granulated sugar

Vegan substitute for 1 egg, prepared

⅔ cup creamy peanut butter

2 teaspoons vanilla extract

10 to 12 ounces vegan semisweet chocolate chips

½ cup peanuts, chopped

Storing in the refrigerator:

Will keep in an airtight container for up to 4 days, or covered tightly in the refrigerator for up to 6 days.

Freezing:

Freeze in airtight containers for up to 4 months. Let defrost in the refrigerator overnight.

Apricot Oatmeal Crumb Bars

Layers of crunchy goodness are filled with a cooked and heavenly apricot filling.

YIELD: 16 BARS | **ACTIVE TIME:** 20 MINUTES | **COOK TIME:** 35 MINUTES | **TOTAL TIME:** 55 MINUTES

Preheat the oven to 350°F.

To make the middle layer: In a small saucepan, combine the water, apricots, coconut sugar, and cornstarch. Cook over medium-high heat until sauce thickens.

Remove from the heat and stir in the coconut. It will thicken even more as it cools. This takes 5 to 10 minutes. Set aside.

To make the crumb mixture: In a large bowl, combine the flour and nondairy butter. Cut the nondairy butter into the flour until it is like a coarse meal.

To this mixture add the oats, brown sugar, and baking soda. Mix well; I use my fingers to really get it well incorporated.

Remove ½ cup of the mixture. Add the nuts to this ½ cup and reserve.

Press the remaining oat mixture into an ungreased 8- or 9-inch square baking pan.

Spread the apricot mixture evenly all over this layer.

Sprinkle the reserved oat mixture all over the apricot mixture. Spread it out evenly and press lightly with your hand.

Bake at for 30 to 35 minutes for a 9-inch square pan or 35 to 40 minutes for an 8-inch square pan. (The 8-inch pan will make your bars a little taller, as in my photo.)

Let the bars cool completely in the pan. After they have cooled, cut around the edges of the bar slab to make sure they are not stuck to the pan. Lift out and place on a cutting board. If it does not lift easily, cut into bars in the pan. Cut three slices in each direction to get 16 bars.

FOR THE MIDDLE LAYER:

¾ cup water

1 cup dried apricots, finely diced

3 tablespoons coconut sugar

1 tablespoon cornstarch

FOR THE CRUMB BASE AND TOPPING:

1 cup whole wheat flour

½ cup (1 stick, 4 ounces) nondairy butter, chilled

1 cup rolled oats

⅔ cup packed brown sugar

¼ teaspoon baking soda

½ cup walnuts, finely chopped

Storing in the refrigerator:

Will keep in the refrigerator for about 5 days.

Freezing:

Freeze in freezer bags for up to 4 months.

Peanut Butter Cup Balls

Who doesn't like a peanut butter cup? Now you can have them at a moment's notice, for yourself or friends. Thank goodness they can be frozen—that will add a little extra layer of protection for overindulgence.

YIELD: 48 CANDIES | **ACTIVE TIME:** 1 HOUR | **COOK TIME:** 1 HOUR | **TOTAL TIME:** 2 HOURS

4 tablespoons nondairy butter, melted

¼ cup creamy peanut butter

2 cups powdered sugar

12 ounces vegan chocolate chips

Mix the melted nondairy butter and peanut butter together. Work in the powdered sugar by hand. It will be pretty stiff but that is good.

Form into 48 balls. (I divide the dough in half, then each half into half, and so on, until I get 48 little chunks. Then I roll them in the palms of my hands). Place in a large bowl.

Refrigerate for about an hour.

Line a cookie sheet with waxed paper. I cut the piece to fit inside the pan so that it lays flat.

Melt the chocolate over a hot water bath or in a double boiler.

Take the peanut butter balls out of the fridge and work with about six at a time. Put the unused balls back in the fridge while you are working.

Roll each ball in the chocolate and pick up with two forks. Lay on the prepared cookie sheet.

When all the balls are coated, place the pan in the refrigerator or freezer to harden up, about an hour.

To serve, you can place each ball in a mini paper cup for looks or just pile in a stack.

I keep them in the refrigerator because the chocolate will get sticky.

Storing in the refrigerator:

Will keep in the refrigerator for a couple of weeks.

Freezing:

Freeze in freezer bags and just take out a few when you want. They will defrost at room temperature within 1 to 2 hours. Will keep for up to 4 months in the freezer.

Chocolate Peppermint Cookie Dough Balls

Sometimes something that is sweet and chocolaty just seems to be necessary. With little effort and without turning on the oven, Chocolate Peppermint Cookie Dough is yours.

YIELD: 42 BALLS | **ACTIVE TIME:** 20 MINUTES | **COOK TIME:** 0 | **TOTAL TIME:** 20 MINUTES

Place all the ingredients into a large bowl. Blend well. Roll into 42 balls and that is it!

- 1½ cups unsalted cashews, ground
- ⅔ cup rolled oats, ground
- ½ teaspoon sea salt
- 1 tablespoon unsweetened cocoa
- 3 tablespoons pure maple syrup
- 2 tablespoons Kahlùa
- 1 teaspoon peppermint extract
- ¼ cup vegan mini chocolate chips
- 1 cup vegan granola (no raisins), ground

Storing in the refrigerator:

Will keep in the refrigerator for 2 weeks.

Freezing:

Freeze in freezer bags and just take one or a few out when you have the craving. They are not frozen hard, so you can actually start enjoying one right away. Will keep in the freezer for up to 4 months.

Kahlúa Truffles

No-bake treats are so easy to make. This recipe has chocolate graham crackers, dates, and a little bit of Kahlúa for an over-the-top taste.

YIELD: 48 TRUFFLES | **ACTIVE TIME:** 20 MINUTES | **COOK TIME:** 1 MINUTE | **TOTAL TIME:** 21 MINUTES

Crush the chocolate graham crackers into fine crumbs or, more easily, put in a food processor and grind. Put the crushed crackers in a large bowl and add the nondairy milk powder.

Stir in the nondairy milk and Kahlúa. Mix until all is moistened. It will be there in less than a minute. Stir in the dates.

Place the ground pecans in a dish and set aside.

Divide the dough in half repeatedly until you have 16 portions of dough. Divide each of these 16 parts into thirds. This will give you 48 portions.

They will be sticky as you divide them, but when you roll them in the palms of your hands, they will not stick at all. Roll each portion into a smooth ball, then roll each ball in the pecans.

All done. Keep them in the refrigerator.

2½ cups ground vegan chocolate graham crackers (about 10 ounces)

¼ nondairy milk powder

½ cup nondairy milk

3 tablespoons Kahlúa

⅔ cup dates, finely chopped

⅓ cup pecans, finely chopped or processed in a food processor

Storing in the refrigerator:

Will keep covered in the refrigerator for up to 2 weeks.

Freezing:

Freeze in airtight containers for up to 4 months. You can actually eat these immediately. Even right out of the freezer.

Carrot Cake Cupcakes

Turn a carrot cake into a cupcake and top it with a frosting . . . or not. That is one way to get your family to eat more vegetables.

YIELD: 12 CUPCAKES | **ACTIVE TIME:** 20 MINUTES | **COOK THME:** 35 MINUTES | **TOTAL TIME:** 55 MINUTES

Preheat the oven to 375°F. Line 12 muffin cups with cupcake liners.

In a medium-size bowl, mix the flours, baking powder, cinnamon, allspice, and nutmeg.

In a large bowl, combine the egg substitute, brown sugar, chocolate chips, coconut oil, and vanilla. Beat well.

Alternately add the flour mixture and nondairy milk to the egg mixture. Fold in the carrot.

Evenly divide the batter among the 12 prepared muffin cups. Bake for 18 minutes, or until a toothpick inserted into the center of a cupcake comes out clean.

Remove from the muffin tin and let cool completely on a wire rack.

To make the icing: With an electric mixer on medium speed, beat the nondairy butter and nondairy cream cheese together. Add the powdered sugar and vanilla. Beat well. Pipe onto the muffins with any decorative tip that you like. Sprinkle a little raw sugar over the tops for decoration.

1 cup all-purpose flour

½ cup whole wheat flour

1½ teaspoons baking powder

1 teaspoon ground cinnamon

¼ teaspoon ground allspice

¼ teaspoon ground nutmeg

Vegan substitute for 2 eggs, prepared

¾ cup packed light brown sugar

½ cup vegan semisweet chocolate chips, melted

⅓ cup coconut oil

1 teaspoon vanilla extract

¼ cup nondairy milk

2 cups carrot, grated (about 5 carrots)

FOR THE ICING:

½ cup (1 stick, 4 ounces) nondairy butter, at room temperature

½ cup nondairy cream cheese, softened

2 cups powdered sugar

1 teaspoon vanilla extract

Raw sugar, for garnish

Storing in the refrigerator:

Will keep covered in the refrigerator for up to 4 days.

Freezing:

Freeze in airtight containers for up to 4 months. Let defrost in the refrigerator overnight and they are ready to serve.

Black Walnut Raisin Bread

Packed full of raisins and black walnuts, this substantial bread can be for breakfast or a snack.

YIELD: 1 LOAF | **ACTIVE TIME:** 15 MINUTES | **COOK TIME:** 50 MINUTES | **TOTAL TIME:** 1 HOUR 5 MINUTES

Preheat the oven to 350°F. Lightly grease an 8½-inch loaf pan with the coconut oil.

In a large bowl, mix together the flours, baking powder, and salt. Add the egg substitute along with the maple syrup, nondairy milk, and nondairy butter. Mix well with an electric mixer on medium speed.

Fold in the walnuts and raisins. Pour into the prepared loaf pan and bake for 50 minutes. Remove from oven and let cool for about 10 minutes, then remove from the pan and let cool completely on a wire rack.

1 tablespoon coconut oil

1½ cups all-purpose flour

½ cup whole wheat flour

1½ teaspoons baking powder

½ teaspoon sea salt

Vegan substitute for 1 egg, prepared

⅓ cup pure maple syrup

¾ cup nondairy milk

3 tablespoons nondairy butter, melted

1 cup black walnuts, chopped

½ cup raisins

Storing in the refrigerator:

Will keep covered in the refrigerator for about 1 week.

Freezing:

Freeze in either resealable plastic bags or a hard-sided freezer container for up to 4 months. Defrost in the refrigerator and serve warm or cold.

Moist and Extravagant Carrot Bundt Cake

Low and slow is how you bake this cake. It is rich with sweetness and loaded with spices. No icing necessary.

YIELD: 1 CAKE; SERVES 16 PEOPLE | **ACTIVE TIME:** 30 MINUTES | **COOK TIME:** 1½ HOURS | **TOTAL TIME:** 2 HOURS

Preheat the oven to 275°F. Grease a Bundt or tube pan with the coconut oil and set aside.

In a medium-size saucepan, combine the carrot, raisins, water, and sugars. Bring to a boil, stirring. Boil at a medium boil for 20 minutes. Remove from the heat and pour into a large bowl.

As it is cooling, stir in the nondairy butter.

In a medium-size bowl, mix together the flours, spices, and baking powder. Add this to the mixture in the large bowl. Mix well and stir in the nuts.

Scoop into the prepared pan and bake for 1½ hours. Remove from the oven and let cool for 10 minutes. With a sharp knife, loosen the cake a bit from the inside column. Check the edges to make sure they are not stuck. Turn over onto a wire rack and let cool completely.

1 tablespoon coconut oil

2½ cups grated carrot

2 cups raisins

2 cups water

1 cup coconut sugar

1 cup granulated sugar

½ cup (1 stick, 4 ounces) nondairy butter

2 cups all-purpose flour

1 cup whole wheat flour

1 teaspoon ground cinnamon

1 teaspoon ground cloves

½ teaspoon ground allspice

2 teaspoons baking powder

1 cup walnuts, chopped

Storing in the refrigerator:

Will keep covered in the refrigerator for 4 to 5 days.

Freezing:

Cut into the largest pieces that will fit in your freezer containers. Freeze in hard-sided freezer containers for up to 3 months. Defrost in the refrigerator and serve.

CHAPTER EIGHT

Always Frozen

Chunky Peanut Butter Ice Cream

It is amazing that you can have ice cream that is dairy-free. Cold, rich, and sweet, this version is packed with crunchy maple peanut butter.

YIELD: 2¾ CUPS ICE CREAM | **ACTIVE TIME:** 5 MINUTES | **ICE-CREAM MAKER TIME:** 20 MINUTES | **TOTAL TIME:** 25 MINUTES

Put the ice cream maker's bucket into the freezer at least 18 hours before making the ice cream.

Mix the peanut butter, 2 tablespoons of the maple syrup, and the peanuts together. Put in a shallow container and place in the freezer. When it is hard enough, take it out of the freezer and break into chunks with a spoon. The chunks will be all different sizes but under a ½-inch. Place back in the freezer while you are making the ice cream.

Place the chilled ice cream bucket in the ice cream maker. Attach the paddle.

Pour the coconut cream in a small bowl and add the remaining 2 tablespoons of maple syrup. Mix well. Pour into the ice cream maker's bucket. Put on the lid and turn on the machine.

After 15 minutes, pour the peanut butter chunks into the ice cream mixture in the machine. If the pieces have become a bit stuck together, break them up as you drop the pieces into the ice cream. Let the machine run for another 5 minutes or so, to incorporate the chunks. Serve immediately as soft-serve or pour into a glass freezer container with a tight-fitting lid and freeze so that you can scoop it out when it becomes hard.

The ice cream will keep in the freezer for much longer than it will be there.

¼ cup creamy peanut butter

4 tablespoons pure maple syrup, divided

¼ cup roasted peanuts

1 (14-ounce) can full-fat coconut cream (17% to 22% fat)

Chocolate Espresso Ice Cream

A little bit of espresso pumps up chocolate to a richer and deeper taste. Add it to coconut cream for an amazing frozen treat.

YIELD: 2¼ CUPS ICE CREAM | **ACTIVE TIME:** 5 MINUTES | **ICE-CREAM MAKER TIME:** 20 MINUTES | **TOTAL TIME:** 25 MINUTES

Put the ice cream maker's bucket into the freezer at least 18 hours before making the ice cream.

Place all the ingredients in a medium-size bowl. Mix well.

Place the chilled ice cream bucket in the ice-cream maker. Attach the paddle.

Pour the ice cream mixture into the ice-cream maker, put on the lid, and turn on the machine.

Let it mix for 15 to 20 minutes. Serve immediately as soft-serve or pour into a glass freezer container with a tight-fitting lid and freeze so that you can scoop it out when it becomes hard.

The ice cream will keep in the freezer for up to 6 months.

1 (14-ounce) can full-fat coconut cream (17% to 22% fat)

1 teaspoon instant espresso stirred into 2 tablespoons hot water

2 teaspoons unsweetened cocoa powder

¼ cup plus 2 tablespoons pure maple syrup

1 teaspoon vanilla extract

Pinch of salt

2 tablespoons vegan chocolate syrup

Almond Butter Cookie Dough Ice Cream

Cookie dough ice cream has become one of the most popular ice creams in the nation since it came on stage about ten years ago. The great thing about this recipe is that all is completely nondairy.

YIELD: 2 CUPS ICE CREAM | **ACTIVE TIME:** 15 MINUTES | **ICE-CREAM MAKER TIME:** 20 MINUTES |
TOTAL TIME: 35 MINUTES

Put the ice cream maker's bucket into the freezer for at least 18 hours before making the ice cream.

To make the cookie dough: Place all the cookie dough ingredients in a medium-size bowl. Mix well and then transfer to a freezer-safe container. Freeze for about an hour, just to make it a little harder.

To make the ice cream: Combine the coconut cream, maple syrup, and salt in a medium-size bowl. Mix well.

Place the chilled ice cream bucket in the ice cream maker. Attach the paddle.

Pour the ice cream mixture into the ice-cream maker, put on the lid, and turn on the machine.

Meanwhile, take the cookie dough out of the freezer. Use a spoon to scrape across the top and make little chunks.

At about the 15-minute point, pour the chunked cookie dough into the ice cream and let it mix throughout. You won't need to go over 20 minutes for mixing. Often 15 minutes is good.

Serve immediately as soft-serve or pour into a glass freezer container with a tight-fitting lid and freeze so that you can scoop it out when it becomes hard.

The ice cream will keep in the freezer for up to 6 months.

FOR THE COOKIE DOUGH:

½ cup almond butter

2 tablespoons pure maple syrup

½ teaspoon vanilla extract

¼ cup all-purpose flour

Pinch sea salt

FOR THE ICE CREAM:

2 (14-ounce) cans full-fat coconut
    cream (17% to 22%)

¼ cup pure maple syrup

Pinch of salt

Chocolate Chip Peppermint Ice Cream

Nothing is better than a nice bowl of peppermint ice cream mixed with a little chocolate. The ice cream is not green because there are no dyes, but it tastes just like the one we had when we were kids.

YIELD: 2 CUPS ICE CREAM | **ACTIVE TIME:** 5 MINUTES | **ICE-CREAM MAKER TIME:** 20 MINUTES | **TOTAL TIME:** 25 MINUTES

Put the ice cream maker's bucket into the freezer for at least 18 hours before making the ice cream.

Combine the coconut cream, maple syrup, peppermint extract, and salt in a medium-size bowl. Mix well.

Place the chilled ice cream bucket in the ice cream maker. Attach the paddle.

Pour the ice-cream mixture into the ice-cream maker, put on the lid, and turn on the machine.

At about the 15-minute point, pour in the chocolate chips and let them mix throughout. You won't need to go over 20 minutes for mixing. Often 15 minutes is good.

Serve immediately as soft-serve or pour into a glass freezer container with a tight-fitting lid and freeze so that you can scoop it out when it becomes hard.

The ice cream will keep in the freezer for 3 to 4 months.

1 (14-ounce) can full-fat coconut cream (17% to 22% fat)

¼ cup pure maple syrup

1 teaspoon peppermint extract

Pinch of salt

2 tablespoons vegan chocolate chips

Chocolate Fudge Ice Cream Pops

These deeply rich pops are cute and chocolaty. A few bites brings such pleasure.

YIELD: 10 POPS | **ACTIVE TIME:** 30 MINUTES | **ICE-CREAM MAKER TIME:** 20 MINUTES | **TOTAL TIME:** 50 MINUTES

Put the ice cream maker's bucket into the freezer at least 18 hours before making the ice cream.

Combine all the ingredients, except the chocolate melts, in a medium-size bowl. Mix well.

Place the chilled ice cream bucket in the ice-cream maker. Attach the paddle.

Pour the ice cream mixture into the ice cream maker, put on the lid and turn on the machine.

Let it mix for 15 to 20 minutes. Transfer to a freezer-safe container so that it can get hard enough for scooping into 1-inch balls. It takes about an hour.

The edges freeze first, so for easier scooping, go ahead and scoop the edges before the whole thing is solid. Stick a pop stick in one end of the ball and place, stick side down, in a short, sturdy glass. Put quite a few in the glass, but not touching, and put the glass in the freezer for the balls to get hard on the sticks. Put the original ice cream back into the freezer to get hard again for more scooping. You may leave the pops in the freezer for a day if you can't get to dipping them the same day.

Melt the chocolate according to the package directions.

When ready to dip, place the chocolate in a narrower glass for ease of dipping. Take a pop and dip straight down to get the whole ball coated with the chocolate. It is not necessary to touch the stick. Place, stick side down, in a short, sturdy glass. Put quite a few in the glass, but not touching, and put the glass in the freezer for the chocolate to harden without the ice cream's melting. When all the pops are coated, transfer to a freezer-safe container with a tight-fitting lid. The container should be large enough so that you can lay the pops down horizontally.

The ice cream pops will keep in the freezer for up to 6 months.

1 (14-ounce) can full-fat coconut cream (17% to 22% fat)

¼ cup unsweetened cocoa powder

3 tablespoons pure maple syrup

1 teaspoon vanilla extract

Pinch of salt

1 cup vegan chocolate melts, for dipping

10 pop/cake sticks

Strawberry Bonbons

Have you ever had bonbons at the movies? Now you can treat yourself special at home. These little balls of chocolate are filled with fruity strawberry ice cream.

YIELD: 30 BONBONS | **ACTIVE TIME:** 30 MINUTES | **ICE-CREAM MAKER TIME:** 20 MINUTES | **TOTAL TIME:** 50 MINUTES

Put the ice cream maker's bucket into the freezer at least 18 hours before making the ice cream.

Combine all of the ingredients, except the chocolate melts, in a medium-size bowl. Mix well.

Place the chilled ice cream bucket in the ice cream maker. Attach the paddle.

Pour the ice cream mixture into the ice cream maker, put on the lid, and turn on the machine.

Let it mix for 15 to 20 minutes. Transfer to a freezer-safe container so that it can get hard enough for scooping into 1-inch balls. It takes about an hour.

The edges freeze first, so for easier scooping, go ahead and scoop the edges before the whole thing is solid. Put the original ice cream back into the freezer to get hard again for more scooping. Place the balls in a separate container and stick into the freezer every few balls so they stay hard. Continue until all of the ice cream is scooped into balls.

Melt the chocolate according to the package directions.

Line two baking sheets with waxed paper and set next to where you are working.

Take the frozen balls out of the freezer and start rolling them very quickly in the melted chocolate. Use two forks to lift and place on one lined baking sheet. Place the baking sheet back in the freezer every so often to keep the ice cream hard. Now you can use the other baking sheet and continue in this process until all the balls are dipped. When all the bonbons are coated, place in a freezer-safe container with a tight-fitting lid.

The ice cream will keep in the freezer for 6 months.

1 (14-ounce) can full-fat coconut cream (17% to 22% fat)

¼ cup frozen strawberries, partially defrosted and chopped, juices reserved

3 tablespoons pure maple syrup

1 teaspoon vanilla extract

Pinch of salt

1 cup vegan chocolate melts, for dipping

Watermelon Citrus Popsicles

This recipe could also be called fruit on a stick. There is nothing in this recipe except three different fruits, and what could be more refreshing or healthier than fruit on a stick?

YIELD: 12 TO 20 POPS, DEPENDING ON YOUR MOLD | **ACTIVE TIME:** 30 MINUTES | **FREEZER TIME:** ABOUT 5 HOURS | **TOTAL TIME:** 5½ HOURS

Cut the watermelon off the rind and then into chunks. Place in a food processor, chopper, or blender. Process until smooth.

After your watermelon is blended, pour it through a sieve. The amount will equal about 4 cups. Do not worry about exact measurement. If you get 6 cups, it will be a pretty sweet pop, but why not. Set aside.

Squeeze all the juice you can out of the grapefruits. Pour this liquid through a sieve also. You want about 2 cups of grapefruit juice. Again, don't stress about exact measurements. Set aside.

Squeeze the juice from the oranges. Put through a sieve; this should measure about 1 cup of orange juice.

Mix all three of the juices together and stir. Pour into you pop molds and freeze for at least 5 hours. The extra juice can be refrigerated in a container until the first batch is frozen.

Take the frozen pops out of the mold and transfer to a freezer bag. Place back in the freezer. Fill the molds with the remaining juice and freeze for at least 5 hours.

They will keep in the freezer for about 2 months.

1 small seedless baby watermelon
2 ruby red grapefruits
2 large oranges

Cherry Apple Pops

Natural fruit flavors are combined to make these easy and refreshing pops. If you have a sweet craving, these pops can always be there in the freezer to satisfy.

YIELD: 6 TO 8 POPS, DEPENDING ON YOUR MOLD | **ACTIVE TIME:** 10 MINUTES | **FREEZER TIME:** ABOUT 5 HOURS |
TOTAL TIME: 5 HOURS 10 MINUTES

Mix both ingredients together and then pour into your molds.

Put in the freezer for about 5 hours to freeze solid. They keep perfectly in the freezer for about 2 months.

2 cups frozen cherries
2 cups unfiltered apple juice

Mixed Fruit Pops

When you just can't decide what fruity flavor will hit the spot, make these pops. There are three fruits; they meld just right.

YIELD: 6 TO 8 POPS, DEPENDING ON YOUR MOLD | **ACTIVE TIME:** 10 MINUTES | **FREEZER TIME:** ABOUT 5 HOURS | **TOTAL TIME:** 5 HOURS 10 MINUTES

Mix all the ingredients together and then pour into your molds.

Put in the freezer for about 5 hours to freeze solid. They keep for about 2 months in the freezer.

1 cup blueberries

1 cup strawberries

2 cups orange juice

¼ cup pure maple syrup

INDEX